Handpicked: *Painting Flowers from 1900 to Today*

written and edited by
Megan Breckell
Naomi Polonsky

with an essay by
Olivia Meehan

Kettle's Yard/University of Cambridge

This publication is generously supported by:
Sally and Edward Benthall
The Finnis Scott Foundation

Rajan Bijlani
Peter and Wendy Blythe
Jenna Burlingham Gallery
John and Jennifer Crompton
Nicholas Crompton
Thomas Dane Gallery
Claire and Martin Daunton
Emma Davis
Stamos J Fafalios
Emily and Matthew Flowers
Sean Gorvy
Sarah and Gerard Griffin
Xavier Hufkens
Richard and Florence Ingleby
Lyndsey Ingram
The Jaccaud Family
Lulu Lytle
Leonie McLaren
Suling C Mead
Andrew Nairne
Maureen Paley
Carlos and Francesca Pinto
Griselda Pollock
Joanna Prior OBE
Jonathan and Nicole Scott
Tiwani Contemporary
Sir David Verey CBE and Lady Verey
and those who wish to remain anonymous

Friends of Kettle's Yard Supporters
Clodagh Barker
Margie Christian
Michael French
Penny Heath
Nicki and Christie Marrian
Nicci Steele-Williams
and those who wish to remain anonymous

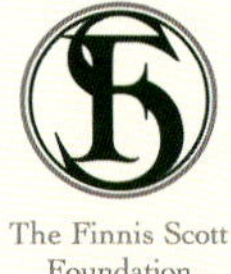

Detail of Caroline Walker,
Kitchen Table, 2025

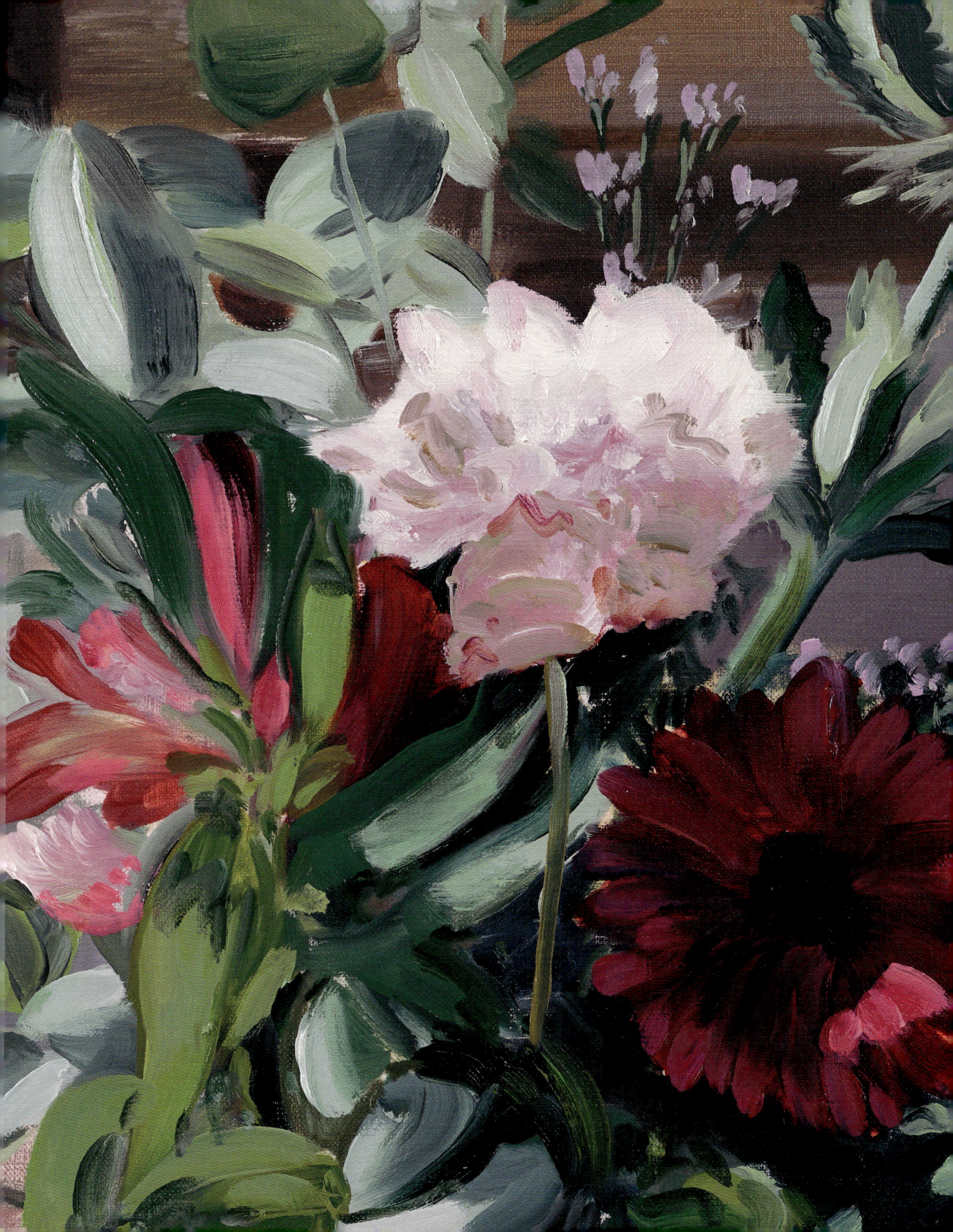

Contents

Foreword

Art is the flower

Charles Rennie Mackintosh (1868–1928), the Scottish architect and artist, famously said: *Art is the flower – Life is the green leaf. Let every artist strive to make his flower a beautiful living thing, something that will convince the world that there may be, there are, things more precious, more beautiful – more lasting than life itself.*

While for Mackintosh art and life were entwined, and the most ambitious art sought to be vital and enduring, the great French painter Henri Rousseau (1844–1910) spoke for many artists when he said: 'Nothing makes me happier than to contemplate nature and to paint it.' Rousseau's *Bouquet of Flowers* (circa 1909–10) and Mackintosh's *Fritillaria* (1915) are among the earliest works in this new anthology of flower paintings from 1900 to today. The flowers and paintings of flowers at Kettle's Yard, Cambridge, are the inspiration for both this book and the related exhibition.

As you wander around the remarkable art-filled former home of Jim and Helen Ede, it is more than likely that you will notice one of the arrangements of fresh cut flowers. Perhaps the bouquet of lime-green tulips in a ceramic jug standing in the dining area; an arrangement of sunny dahlias on the low table close to Jim Ede's bed; a dramatic red peony in the small, stout vase near Helen Ede's Bechstein piano. The flowers create visual correspondences with surrounding artworks, including Winifred Nicholson's *Cyclamen and Primula* (circa 1923) and Christopher Wood's *Flowers* (1930).

Handpicked: Painting Flowers from 1900 to Today brings together the work of 46 artists. It celebrates the astonishing beauty, resonance and importance of flower paintings of the past century and a quarter. It aims to show how a seemingly innocent painting of a flower posy might stand in for the most intense human emotions and experiences or provide the setting for transformative artistic innovations. Across 125 years, artists have constantly reinvigorated one of the oldest genres in art, from the early Modernism of Vanessa Bell (1879–1961) to new and experimental approaches by artists working today, including Bianca Raffaella, Cassi Namoda and Hurvin Anderson.

For this new publication, we are delighted that Olivia Meehan accepted our invitation to write a special essay discussing the history and context of flower painting and some of the relationships to be found between these wonderfully diverse and distinct artworks.

For Jim and Helen Ede, taking time to look closely at a painting of flowers had equal value to observing the flowers that surround us, and each enriched the experience of the other. Art always has the potential to change the way we see. We hope that after seeing the paintings in *Handpicked*, you will see flowers and your world differently.

Megan Breckell and Naomi Polonsky

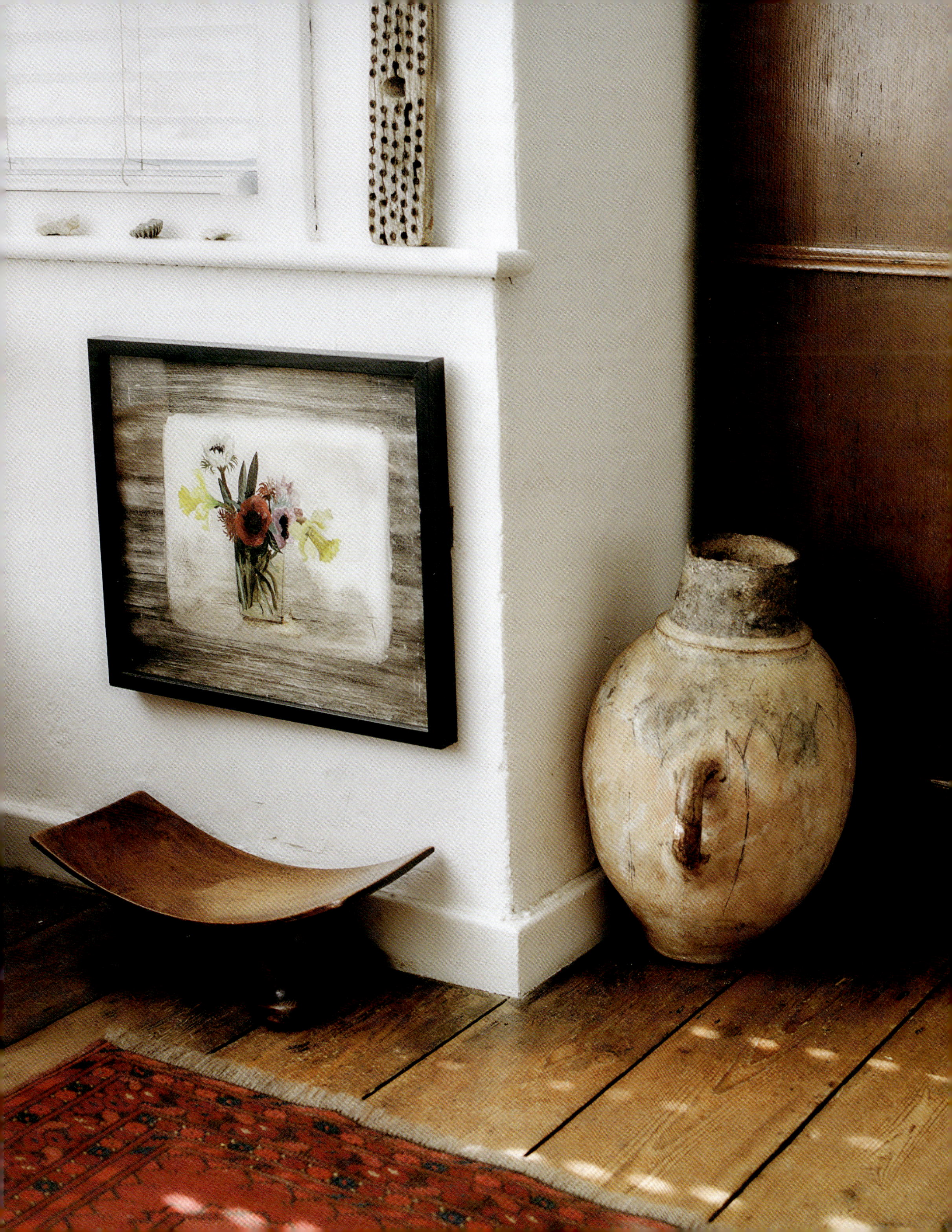

The Essay

Taking the deep snow of flowers for a pillow…

The velvety texture of a rose petal belies its fragility; one small move could destabilise it, causing a separation from the flower itself. How delicate and ephemeral such beauty is, exposing a complex web of initial attraction and inevitable loss. Flower paintings render a short-lived moment, condensing love with the foreseeable pain that accompanies the end of something exquisite. Towards the late 1800s flower painting began to enjoy a gaze different from the one cast upon still-life painting of the 1600s when its fate as a genre was always to linger at the bottom of the hierarchy of painting. Breaking free from the boundaries established by the academy, artists started to experiment with composition and emotion in order to summon a different atmosphere in their paintings of flowers. Taking inspiration from past tradition, along with current concerns and interests, they managed to elicit renewed outcomes in their work.

The quietude evoked in still-life painting is offset by an artful liveliness. The gently arresting sensation to lean in and take a closer look at the details of a seventeenth-century Dutch still-life painting is testament to the masterful skill of the painter. Carefully arranged objects such as fruit, insects and cut flowers were bestowed upon the canvas to convey moral messages of pleasure, life and death; *vanitas, memento mori, nature morte*. Their seeming banality, with a pinch of excess and a touch of realism so effective that the ladybird crawling across the cabbage looks like it might fly away any moment, was a sign of the social standing, wealth but also humility of the commissioner. The painting of flowers and plants has endured across millennia, cultures and techniques. From impulses as different as classifying and identifying the botanical characteristics of flowers to recording the pure pleasure of their beauty and wonder, still-life and flower painting has continued in some form through successive art movements. Whether appreciated for their symbolism, seasonal appeal, architectural form, sculptural quality, specimen type or unique colour, flowers have long played a role in the practice of many artists.

For the viewer the presence of wildflowers, cut flowers and garden flowers in painting may suggest a feeling of summer or spring, a new beginning, nascent promise. Regardless of the artist's intention there is often a universal sense of optimism or love found in painted flowers. In the Victorian era, floriography – the secret language of flowers – offered a way of expressing love, respect, remembrance, friendship or jealousy in coded ways through the type of flower,

Detail of Bianca Raffaella,
Waxflower, 2025

its colour and presentation. Whether a flower pinned to the right or the left lapel, the orientation of the bouquet, a paper flower or a ring engraved with forget-me-nots, it all conveyed meaning between the sender and the recipient. The ability to read that which is hidden in plain sight became a practice performed between lovers and connoisseurs.

A modern arrangement

The kind of newness discoverable in modern flower painting emerges from the multifaceted shifts taking place elsewhere: in literature, language, ideas, politics and technological innovation. The flower as a metaphor for the various stages of love and desire, sorrow and grief, spans the centuries. It was in the final decades of the late nineteenth century that a significant pull away from Realism occurred with the arrival of Impressionism, freeing the artist to explore the notion of nature and the behaviour of flowers and plants in new ways. Most notably, it was in the conjuring of atmosphere that emanates not only from the artists' close observation, but also from the actual vibration and sensation associated with flowers that these changes evolved. In *Handpicked: Painting Flowers from 1900 to Today*, the quiet vivacity of Édouard Vuillard's *Pot de grès et fleurs*, circa 1900–10, and Bianca Raffaella's delicate *Waxflower*, 2025, though created a century apart, each reflect this liberation from the requirement for exactitude.

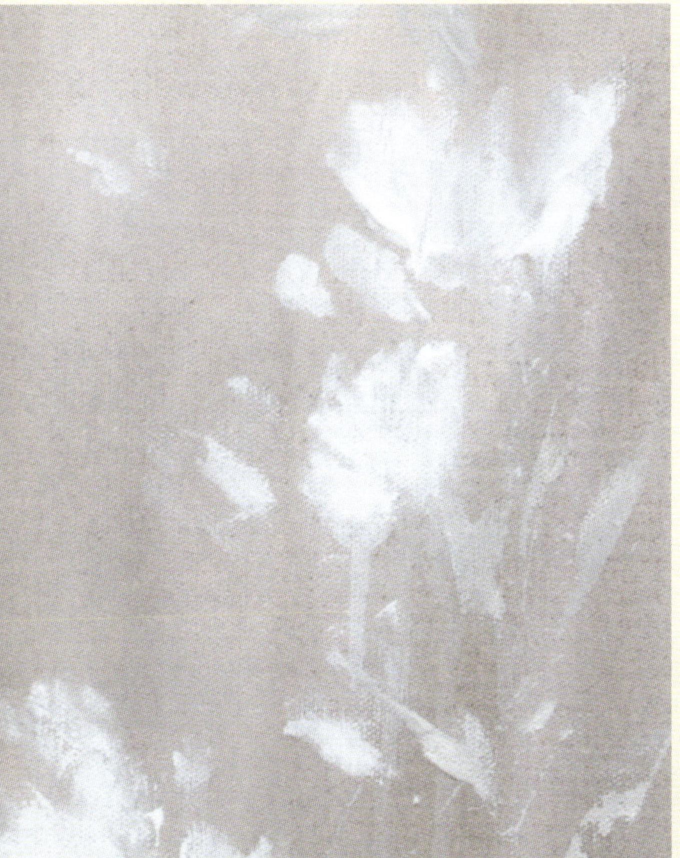

It is in this atmosphere that Virginia Woolf surrounds Mrs Dalloway, in her 1925 novel of the same name, in flowers, masses of cut flowers, at Mulberry's florist: 'delphiniums, sweet peas, bunches of lilac; and carnations, masses of carnations. There were roses; there were irises ... and dark and prim the red carnations, holding their heads up; and all the sweet peas spreading in their bowls, tinged violet, snow white, pale—'. The flowers Mrs Dalloway encounters each have their discrete characteristics, whether in form or colour. From the height of the delphinium to the sprawling sweet peas to the 'nodding tufts of lilac', the flower shop is one huge arrangement in and of itself. Flowers also recur throughout Woolf's novel *The Waves* (1931) as a leitmotif for the main characters, and as a mechanism for immersing the reader into fantastic sensorial sequences.

Woolf's sister Vanessa Bell's painting *Still-life of Dahlias, Chrysanthemums and Begonias*, 1912, portrays vibrant late summer blooms snugly bunched into a painted vase. The loose yet deliberate brushstrokes contradict the tightly packed areas of the composition; crisp outlines nuzzle against soft blurred patches of apricot, pink and mint. The distinctive geometric pattern on the vase is part of a design vocabulary associated with the Omega Workshops, an enterprise established by Bell and her friends in 1913. The profusion of flower heads appears bulky and heavy, while their stems are concealed. The pattern around the vase helps to balance the composition. Bell has cast a spirited charm on the work by way of the cheery flowers, the lively background and the slightly raised angle of the viewer. In contrast Christopher Wood's *The White Vase*, 1930, presents an arrangement of considered harmony in which our gaze is level with the display. The luminous vase delicately holds a spring bunch, with petals pointing upwards like small beacons, opening in a reserved yet elegant manner. The work recalls Henri Rousseau's *Bouquet of Flowers*, circa 1909-10, in which the bouquet is set magnificently before a fabric backdrop. It is composed in such a way that the flowers appear ready to take their final curtain call. This touch of theatricality bestows a certain formal quality upon the painting; it subtly suggests that the flowers might be an ensemble of talented luminaries preparing to conclude a stunning performance. Such seemingly small yet powerful pictorial devices amplify the modernity of flower painting in the early twentieth century.

When the artist-plantsman Cedric Morris set about breeding his own irises, he did so with horticultural wisdom and an artist's eye. *Irises and Tulips*, painted

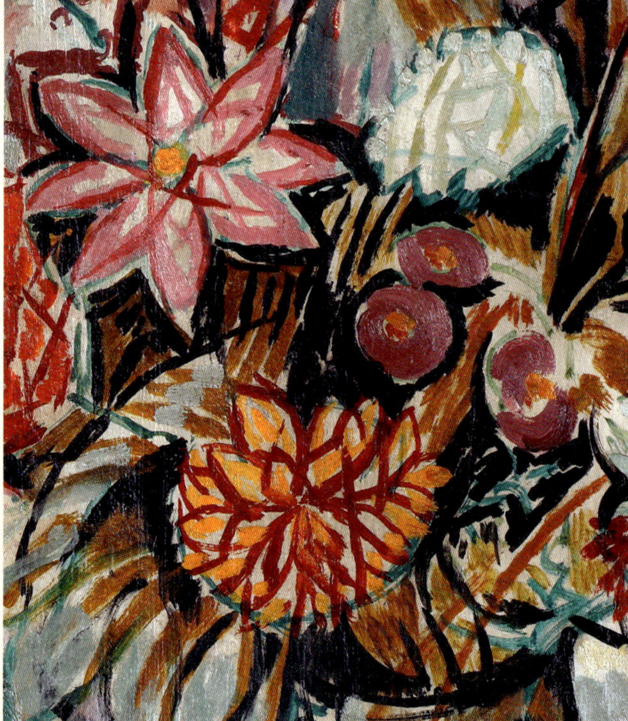

Detail of Vanessa Bell,
Still-life of Dahlias,
Chrysanthemums and Begonias, 1912

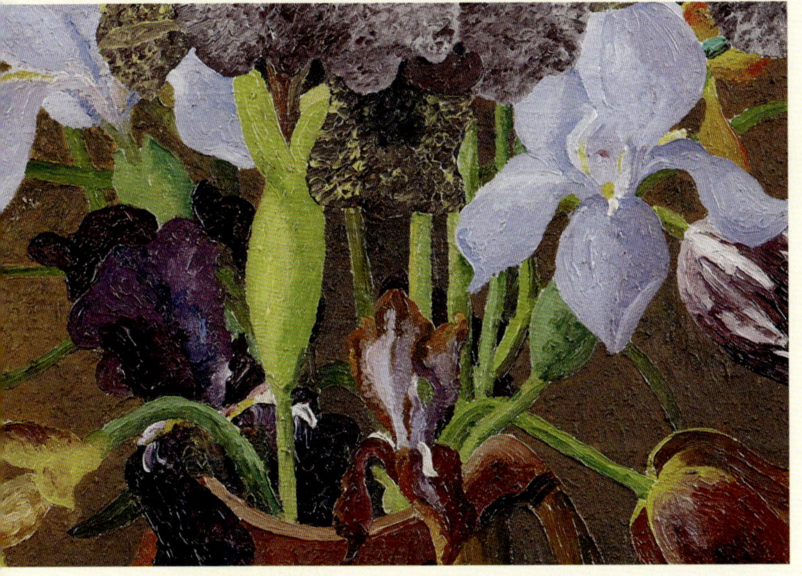

Detail of Cedric Morris, *Irises and Tulips*, 1935

in 1935 when Morris and his partner Arthur Lett-Haines were living in the countryside after stints in Paris and London, demonstrates his ability to capture the fragility and strength of flowers. In the garden bed, irises command full attention and sun, they do not prefer companions, and yet Morris has compelled them to share this portrait space. He discloses the characteristics and personalities of the breeds with simple yet powerful painterly gestures. In this sense Morris captures the temperament of each cultivar, not as an exercise to show the anatomy of the flower, nor to convey a hidden message, but rather to indicate something more like the spirit of a portrait.

On beauty and transience

The life cycle of a flower appears to be fleeting. While the flowering is only one part of a greater sequence, the whole process is an act of transience, and this takes time. Consider how many phases of the moon, how many millilitres of water or hours of sun before the moment of full bloom will occur? Given the time, effort and energy to arrive at the moment of flourishing, to have it pass so swiftly seems cruel. The flower plays a role in a greater ecosystem. Time does not pass in linear fashion; it is part of a cosmological charter. The artist works to capture the essence of the flower but can only ever describe one aspect of what is a multifaceted period of flowering. Even when working from memory, the artist is engaged in a transitory flow of feelings and emotions.

What takes place when a flower is cut from a plant? What cost is it to nature to want to preserve and hold close such beauty? By picking a flower we might appear to end its life, or is it merely a premature beginning to the end of the cycle? Flower arrangements are picked for display in interiors, a nosegay, a lapel, garlands. In Japan, flower arranging is known as *kadō*

(花道 the way of flowers), also referred to as *ikebana*. This practice has evolved over millennia but has always been a means for underscoring humanity in nature, reminding us that beauty is fleeting.

The art critic and writer Okakura Kakuzō (岡倉 覚三) wrote one of the first treatises on Japanese tea culture to appear in English, *The Book of Tea*, published in 1906. He devotes a chapter to the important regard for flowers in the Japanese tearoom, writing of the Master of Flowers:

He respects the economy of nature, selects his victims with careful foresight, and after death does honour to their remains ... When the flower fades, the master tenderly consigns it to the river or carefully buries it in the ground. Monuments even are sometimes erected to their memory.

Gratitude is expressed towards the flower not only for its beauty but ultimately for its sacrifice. The reverence for cut flowers and small planted flowers is an acknowledgement of how they enhance the lives not only of those who observe them but those who nurture and select them for display. For every arrangement there is a shared story of beauty and love. Painting flowers demands a similar devotion of attention. The picture is an outcome of a communion between the artist and the subject, which is often time-based and fragile.

Alison Watt's flawless work *Lying Down*, 2025, projects a quiet and tender beauty. Watt manages to create an atmosphere that is at once weightless and yet heavy in feeling. The pale pink of the petals conjures the blush-painted cheeks in Jean-Auguste-Dominique Ingres's 1806 portrait of Mademoiselle Caroline Rivière, or the rosy interior of a conch or scallop shell. The shadow of the rose lingers below like a ghostly presence; it works to create the impression of the flower gently suspended in the atmosphere.

The single flower portrait set against a solid-coloured background cuts a striking

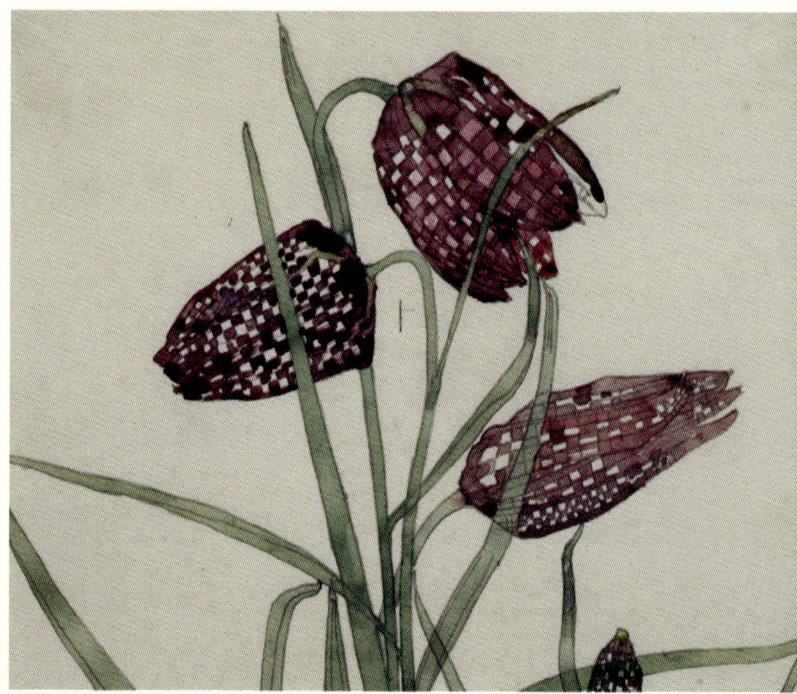

Detail of
Charles Rennie Mackintosh,
Fritillaria, 1915

figure. Summoning the fastidiousness found in botanical illustration, Rory McEwen's *Tulip (Helen Josephine)*, 1975, is powerful and brilliant. The lustrous effect of the watercolour on vellum gives the tulip head depth and dimension, almost lifting it from the page, yet without the trace of a shadow. The snakehead fritillary in Charles Rennie Mackintosh's pencil and watercolour on paper, *Fritillaria*, 1915, accurately resembles the chequered patterning of this flower, with a clear nod to his own architectural designs. To achieve a likeness may be just one facet of flower portraiture and is almost always informed by artistic style.

Of love and intimacy

Within the realm of the quotidian, flowers appear in garden beds, pots, vases and sinks. The seasonal ritual of anticipating, of gathering, pairing and arranging requires a certain keenness of observation and practice. Can flower-arranging ascend to the rarefied realm of domestic etiquettes or does it belong with housekeeping duties? Often regarded as harbingers of joy, flowers are also considered a luxury item reserved for special occasions or associated with abundance and excess. In practice, the domain of flower-arranging lands within multiple spaces and engages different concentrations of labour and care. The Swiss-French architect Le Corbusier considered nature, trees and in particular flowers as part of the geometric and structural fabric of living and dwelling, not for mere decoration. In the domestic space flowers can be arranged to correspond with objects and the people who move around them, like companion planting in the garden or in nature.

Caroline Walker's *The Kitchen Table*, 2025, is arresting precisely because it is a painting not a photograph. It depicts a touching moment of domestic bustle and making. Light from the nearby window touches the top of the child's head and with equal measure it hits the silvery green eucalyptus leaves that stretch tall in the vase of flowers at the centre of the canvas. Patches of bright light anoint everyday objects with electric force. This creates the effect of a glittering atmosphere that seems to emerge from inside the painting itself. The surface of the table is busy with domestic objects. Curiously, the prominent placement of the vase of flowers in the composition does not indicate a hierarchy of importance; rather it positions things to create balance and harmony. The tray of colour markers, the turquoise candle holder and the open orange scissors pointing towards the cuttings are brought together seamlessly. The incidental companionship between these objects and the artist's daughter at the kitchen table makes for a compelling and loving portrait of daily life.

The subject of Aubrey Levinthal's painting *Tulip Nightstand* (*Night*), 2023, prompts a feeling of stillness somehow interrupted or intruded upon. There is a discreet intimacy connected to nightstands; they occupy a personal and restful space in the home. A warm diffused glow pulses around the window in contrast to the translucent black of the vase and the pair of spectacles on the nightstand. With their suggestion of transience, the cool lilac of the tulips and the water in the drinking glass break the sparseness of the scene. Flower paintings may harbour expressions of the love and intimacy that can thrive in a domestic dwelling. In Winifred Nicholson's paintings of flowers, the arrangements are often afforded a view to the outside. Eric Ravilious sets a vase of flowers on a table across from a picture of flowers pinned to the wall opposite (*Ironbridge Interior*, 1941). Such still-life compositions may be read as acts of love towards the subject.

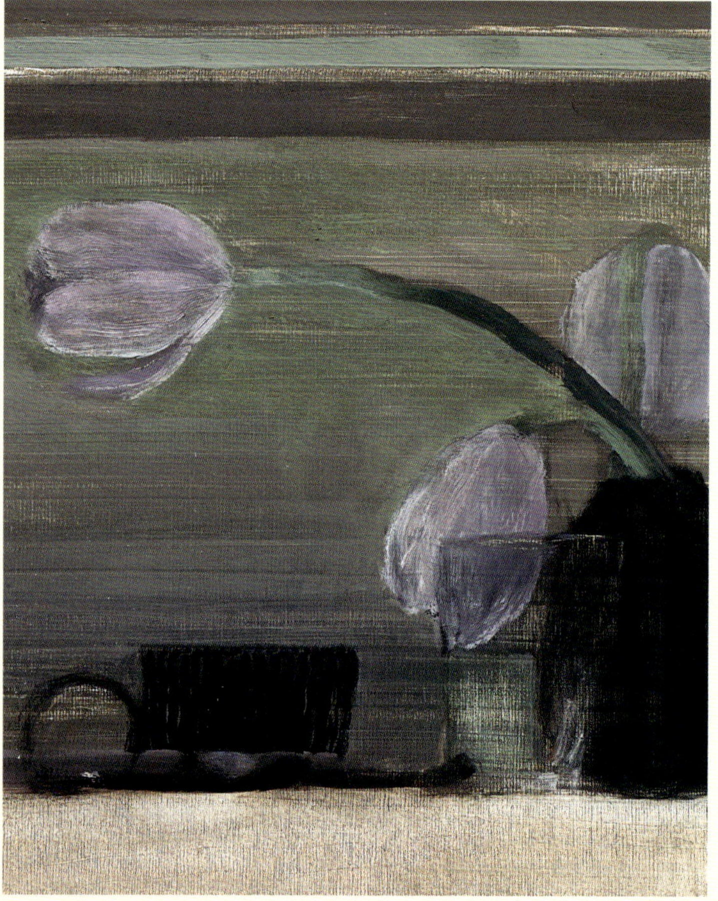

Intimacy in flower painting may also be stated in grander, more exacting gestures. Gluck was inspired by the unique arrangements of Constance Spry. Following a flirtation that spanned the time it took Gluck to meticulously paint a bouquet with flowers supplied by Spry's shop, a courtship began. Gluck sought a perfectionism in painting that was utterly modern. *Convolvulus*, painted in 1940, after the affair with Spry, depicts the flowers otherwise known as bindweed or morning glory. They are placed in a tall glass vessel with a wide opening; tendrils cascade from the lip of the vase while the heads

Detail of Aubrey Levinthal,
Tulip Nightstand (Night), 2023

Detail of Gluck, *Convolvulus*, 1940

trumpet outwards in all directions, underscored by bright heart-shaped leaves and several tightly furled buds. As Gluck pushes the arrangement to the forefront of the canvas, the shiny reflective surface of the marble table and the evenness of the powder-blue backdrop bring a crispness to the picture. The custom-made frames with their 'stepped' effect did not project the paintings forwards – rather they were an invitation to step into the work.

Modern and contemporary flower portraits acknowledge the painstaking traditions of the past but bring to light new and intricate approaches to the field. Most significantly they offer an opportunity for contemplation and reflection. There is a bittersweet notion of the flower painting as something nostalgic, symbolic or scientific. Through the lens of Modernist principles and a contemporary outlook on nature that demands a responsibility for its care, there is scope for experimentation in painterly expression.

Taking the time to describe a painting may feel elementary, and yet it is a complex, lengthy and rewarding exercise that begs the sort of close looking that helps us build rapport with a work of art. The poet, ceramicist and Buddhist nun Ōtagaki Rengetsu (太田垣 蓮月1791-1875) noted the sensations she experienced on her long walks in nature. Slow observation of painting may bring us a step closer to an immersive and thought-provoking experience with art. Following the transient moment when the cherry blossom had fallen from their branches, Rengetsu wrote:

Beneath a tree
taking the deep snow of flowers
for a pillow…

Olivia Meehan

Hurvin Anderson

Born 1965

Dramatic red and blue forms appear rhythmically in Hurvin Anderson's painterly reimagining of floral wallpaper. The graphic pattern includes areas where the blue pigment has become marbled with the white and grey paint underneath, creating the impression that the wallpaper is being seen through a mirror. Anderson often draws on experiences and memories from his early life, as well as recreating places of personal and cultural significance. In *Untitled*, the floral motifs emerge and fade as if the pattern were a distant memory.

Anderson's process germinates organically, starting with a photograph which then becomes a series of drawings and gradually accumulates into a body of work. Through his depiction of patterns, fabrics and materials in domestic settings, Anderson explores his Afro-Caribbean heritage, as well as his experiences of space, identity and community. Plants and foliage are prominent within his wider practice, appearing in real or imagined Caribbean and British landscapes that critically engage with the postcolonial Atlantic world. These compositions provoke ideas surrounding loss of innocence and the consequences of ecological exploitation.

Representations of wallpaper have been prominent in Anderson's work throughout his artistic career. *Untitled* possesses the static quality of a photograph, but the fluidity of the paint is evident in the metallic grey background, which occasionally merges with the reds and blues of the floral pattern. The realm of the home is hinted at but not made explicit: there is no figure, furniture or domestic ephemera. Absence therefore becomes as important as presence – an exploration of the line between that which exists in the world and that which is seen in the mind's eye. *MB*

Untitled, 2025
Acrylic and pigment on paper laid on board
42 x 58 cm
Courtesy the artist and Thomas Dane Gallery

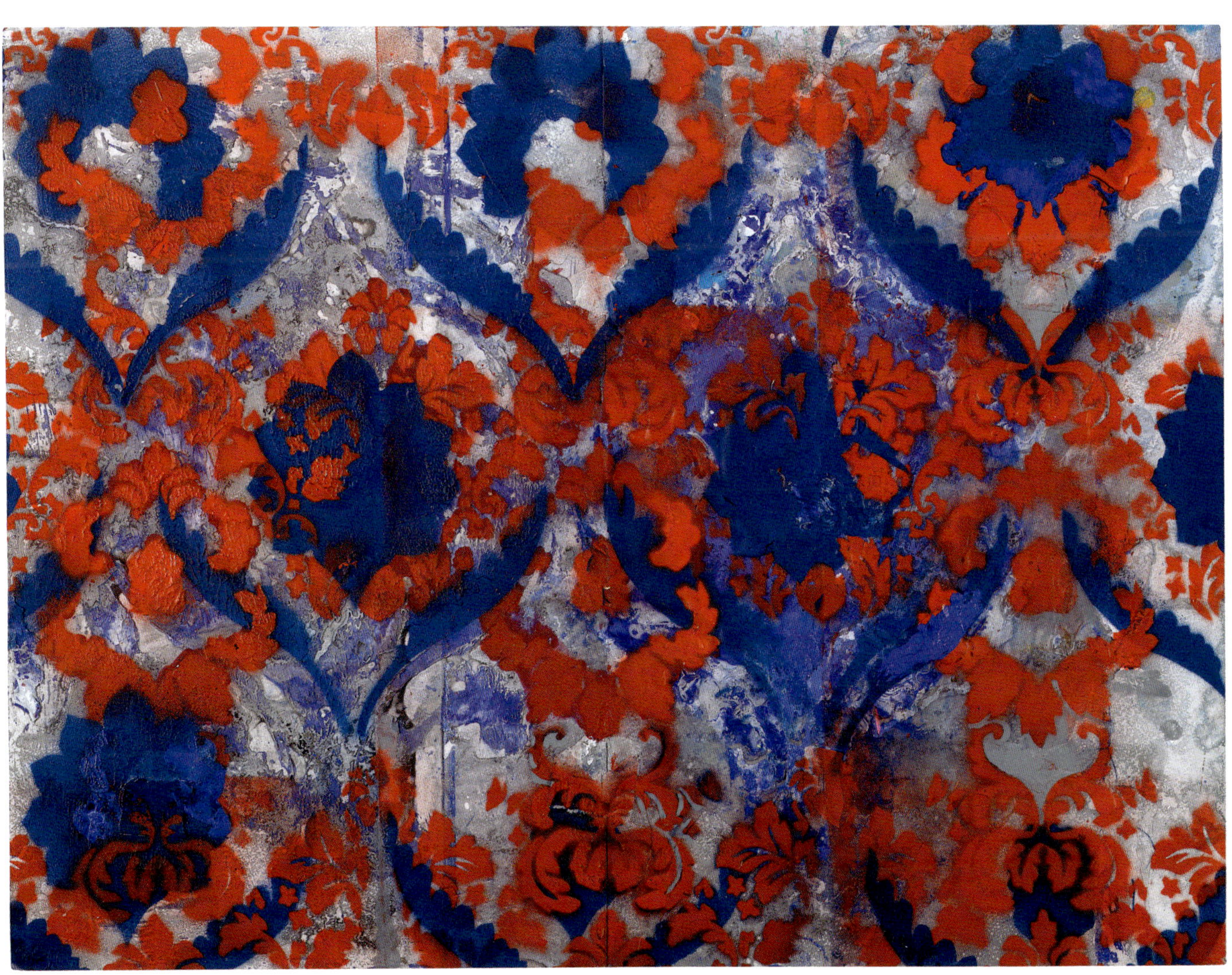

Vanessa Bell
1879–1961

The flowers are the dramatic centrepiece of this composition, their bursts of colour emerging from stark black shadows. Vibrant pinks, reds and oranges, applied in layers of thick paint, suggest clusters of dahlia petals. Crosshatching, a technique that came to be distinctive of Bell's design and decorative work, creates the impression that the flowers are being seen from multiple perspectives simultaneously.

Still-life of Dahlias, Chrysanthemums and Begonias marks a radical shift in Bell's work when she began experimenting with abstract and Cubist forms. Roger Fry's 1910 exhibition *Manet and the Post-Impressionists*, held at the Grafton Galleries, was the catalyst for Bell's engagement with European avant-garde ideas of painting. Like many artists at that time, she began to create works centred on form and colour, inspired by artists such as Paul Cézanne and Henri Matisse. The flowers in this painting are characterised by graphic shapes and expressive marks, suggestive of the early Cubist and Post-Impressionist works she would have seen in Fry's exhibition and on her travels in Europe in the early 1910s.

This painting was created during a two-month stay at Asham House in Sussex in the late summer of 1912, perhaps recording the final bloom of flowers before autumn set in. During this time, Bell painted views of the surrounding landscape and interiors of the house, as well as portraits and still lifes. Two of these paintings were included in *The Second Post-Impressionist Exhibition* at the Grafton Galleries later the same year. Although *Still-life of Dahlias, Chrysanthemums and Begonias* was not one of them, it shows the direction Bell would take in her work following the exhibition, not only in painting but also in her textile, ceramic and interior designs. *MB*

Still-life of Dahlias, Chrysanthemums and Begonias, 1912
Oil on board laid on panel
73 x 51.7 cm
Private collection, care of
Philip Mould & Company

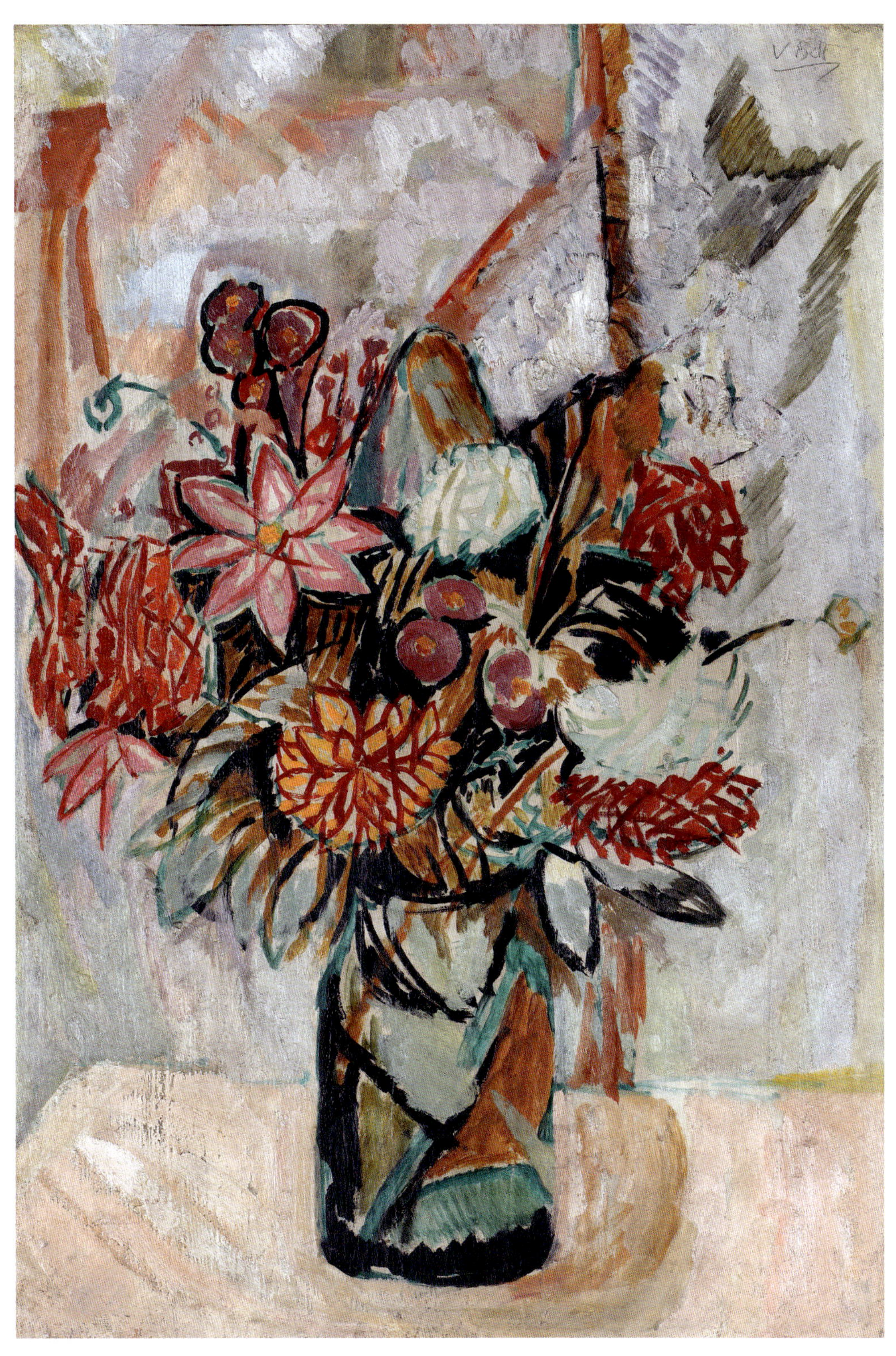

David Bomberg
1890–1957

A plain glass vase can barely contain the shooting stems and blooms that seem to be bursting out of the canvas in David Bomberg's painting. The vase offers a moment of stillness within the exuberant display of vertical brushstrokes. The flowers merge into a radiant backdrop of colour: green, plum, and warm yellow-ochre.

Flowers is one of a series of flower paintings Bomberg made in 1943. Then in his 50s, the artist's early reputation as a leading figure of Vorticism (1914-15), a high point of radical art, had long dissipated. Moving away from energised, hard-edged angular forms, Bomberg had shifted his focus to figurative portraits and landscapes, drawn from nature. However, following a commission as a war artist in 1942, he was rejected from receiving further work for being 'too imaginative'. At the same time, he was repeatedly turned down for teaching posts, which caused him to become increasingly dejected. In an attempt to help him overcome his depression, his wife Lilian brought home some flowers and encouraged him to paint again. This led to a remarkable group of paintings which possess a vivid and unfinished quality, as if they were still in the process of being made. According to Lilian, Bomberg 'wasn't interested in flower arrangement – he just put them in and painted them'.

Created at the height of the Second World War, this painting has been seen to echo the conflict with its 'explosive' mark making and use of colour. An apparently simple subject becomes a means for Bomberg to express the intensity of his feelings in paint and to capture forever the vitality of flowers, offering a timeless response to the violence of the world around him. *AN*

Flowers, 1943
Oil on canvas
76 x 66.2 cm
Leeds Museums and Galleries
(Leeds Art Gallery). Bequeathed
by Leslie Cohen, 2001

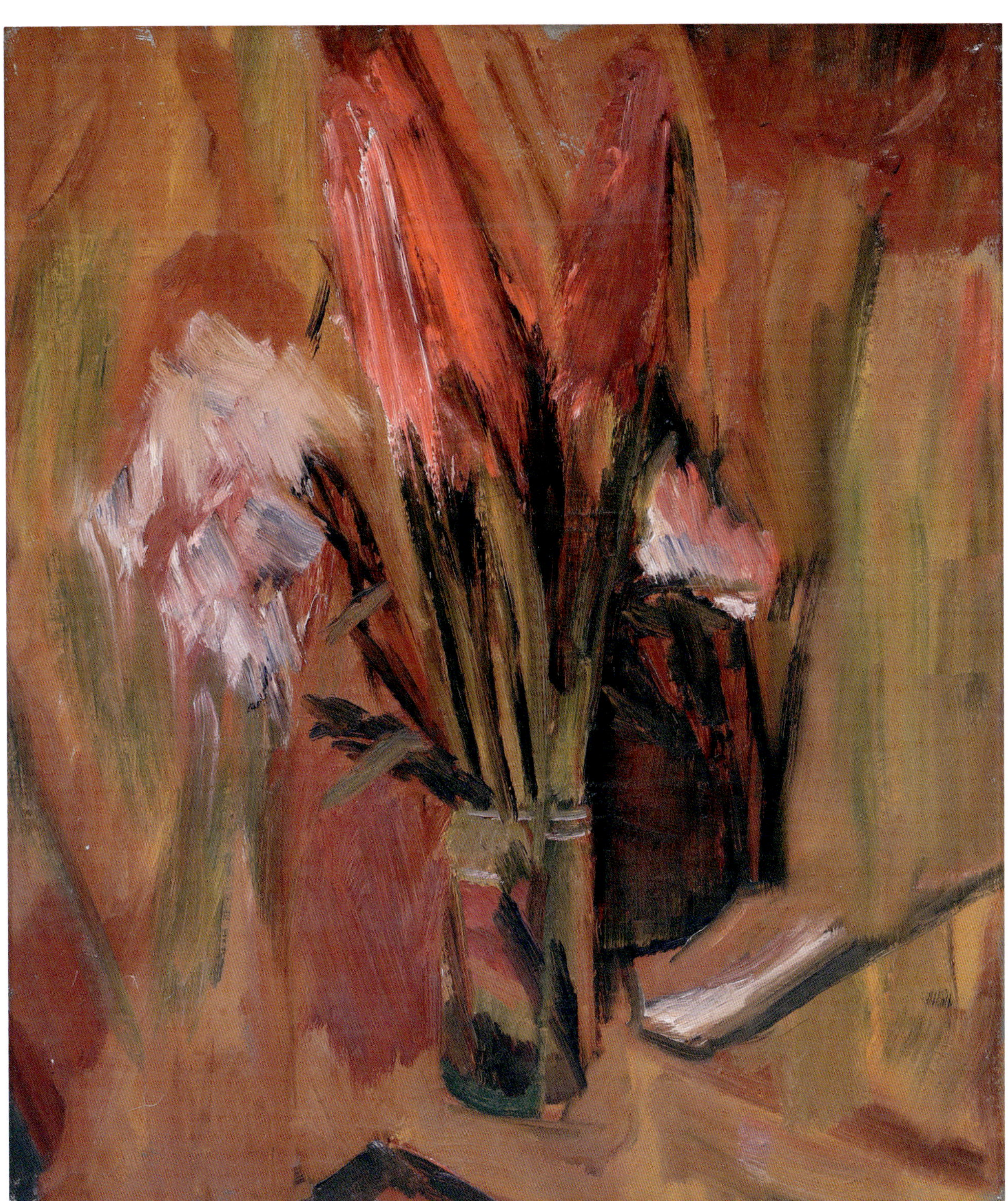

Louise Bourgeois
1911–2010

Frantic marks in pencil and watercolour make up the form of a blue flower in Louise Bourgeois's *La Fleur bleue*. In some areas the paint is watery and loose, in others dry and scratchy, suggesting that the artist did not pause to replenish her paintbrush. The top of the flower extends past the edge of the etching, as though bursting out of the constraints of the page. The whole composition has a febrile energy and intensity.

Bourgeois created a vast range of works over the course of her life, from small fabric drawings to monumental bronze sculptures. She is best known for her spider sculptures, dedicated to her mother. Often biographical, Bourgeois's works interrogate her experiences of childhood, family, gender and sex. Flowers had a deep personal resonance for Bourgeois. In her old age, she could still recall the exact types of flowers grown by her family in the Parisian suburb of Choisy-le-Roi where she grew up. In an early self-portrait, *Reparation* (1945), she represented herself as a young girl bringing a bouquet of white flowers to a family grave.

In the years leading up to her death, Bourgeois returned repeatedly to images of flowers. She said: 'flowers mean new life; they let us forget about death.' Working at the simple butcher-block table in her New York home and studio, she created dozens of floral compositions in rapid succession. Her flowers often expand across the page in watery blooms of red paint. In *La Fleur bleue*, however, there is a sense of wiry tension. The pencil under-drawing, executed in thick dark lines, resembles a tangle of spiders' legs. This painting is not just a representation of a flower, but a symbol of Bourgeois herself, and her life's work. ***NP***

La Fleur bleue, 2007
Watercolour, pencil and etching on paper
20.6 x 28.9 cm
Private collection

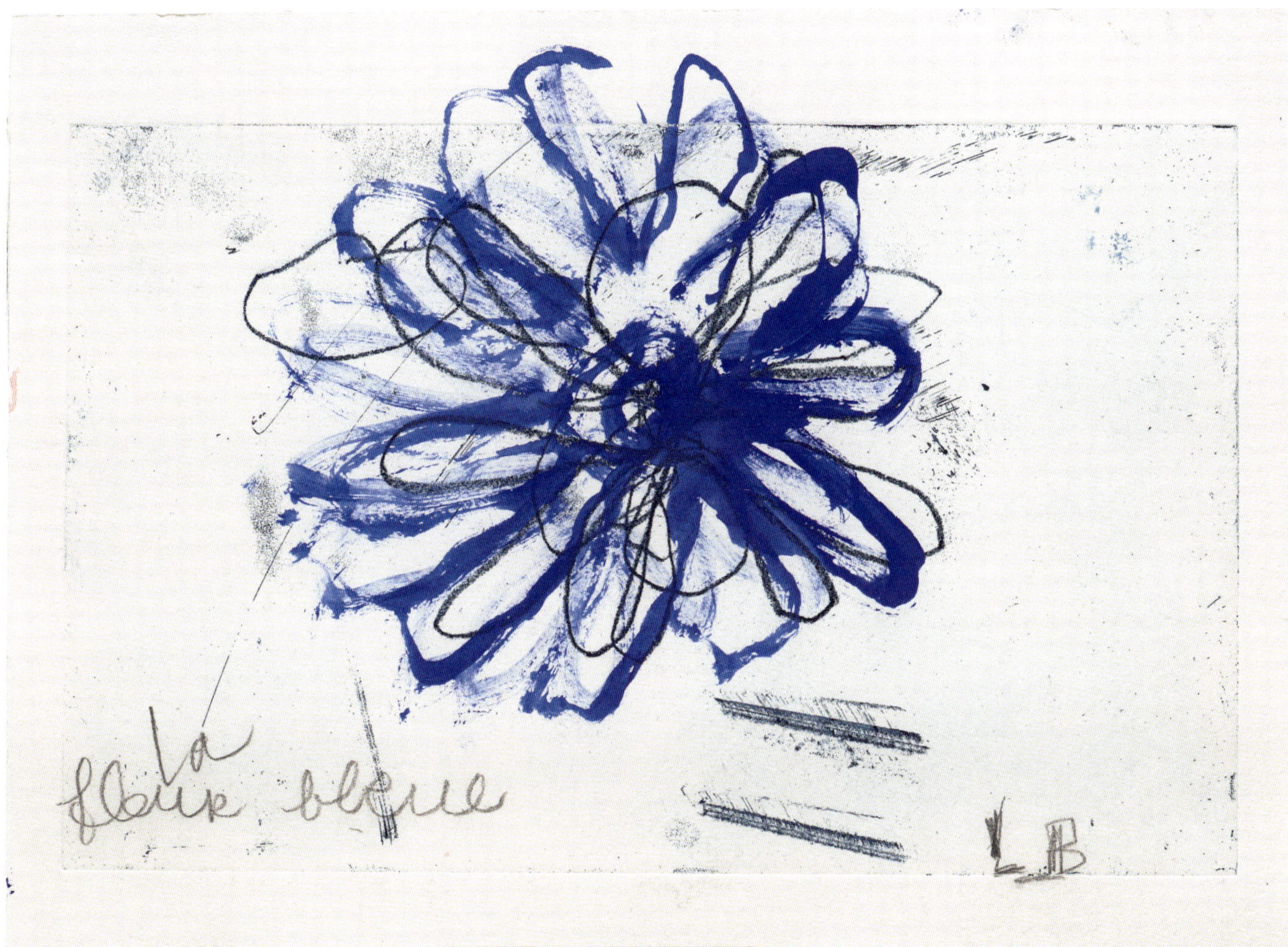
la
fleur bleue
LB

Jai Chuhan

Born 1955

Jai Chuhan's vigorous, energetic flower painting was created in a single sitting in her studio – a rare example of the artist working directly from life. There is an obscure patchwork of other canvases in the background. The organic floral shapes contrast with the architectural space of the studio, but the subject and setting are united by the rich vibrancy of colour: intense reds, deep blues and luminous pinks. Chuhan's impressionistic, impasto painted flowers embody personal memories, art historical references and ecological concerns, accumulated by the artist over the course of her life.

While much of Chuhan's work focuses on human figures in interiors and cityscapes, flowers have appeared in her paintings throughout her artistic career. As a young child she was captivated by Claude Monet's paintings of waterlilies which she encountered at the National Gallery in London soon after she moved to the UK from India. She has often depicted flowers alongside postcards and domestic ephemera, pointing to their role as an adornment in the home. They are also included in her depictions of pregnant women, referencing the floral bouquets given in celebration of a baby's birth, as well as symbolising the cyclical nature of life.

Inspired by examples across the history of art, from Indian miniatures to Francis Bacon, Chuhan explores the ability of flowers to encapsulate different experiences of time. She believes that humans are innately drawn to flowers, saying, 'I think we are hardwired to be attracted to the bright colours and shapes. They are incredibly important for their symbolism, their beauty, their transitory nature.' ***MB***

Flowers II, 2008
Oil on canvas
91 x 77 cm
Courtesy the artist

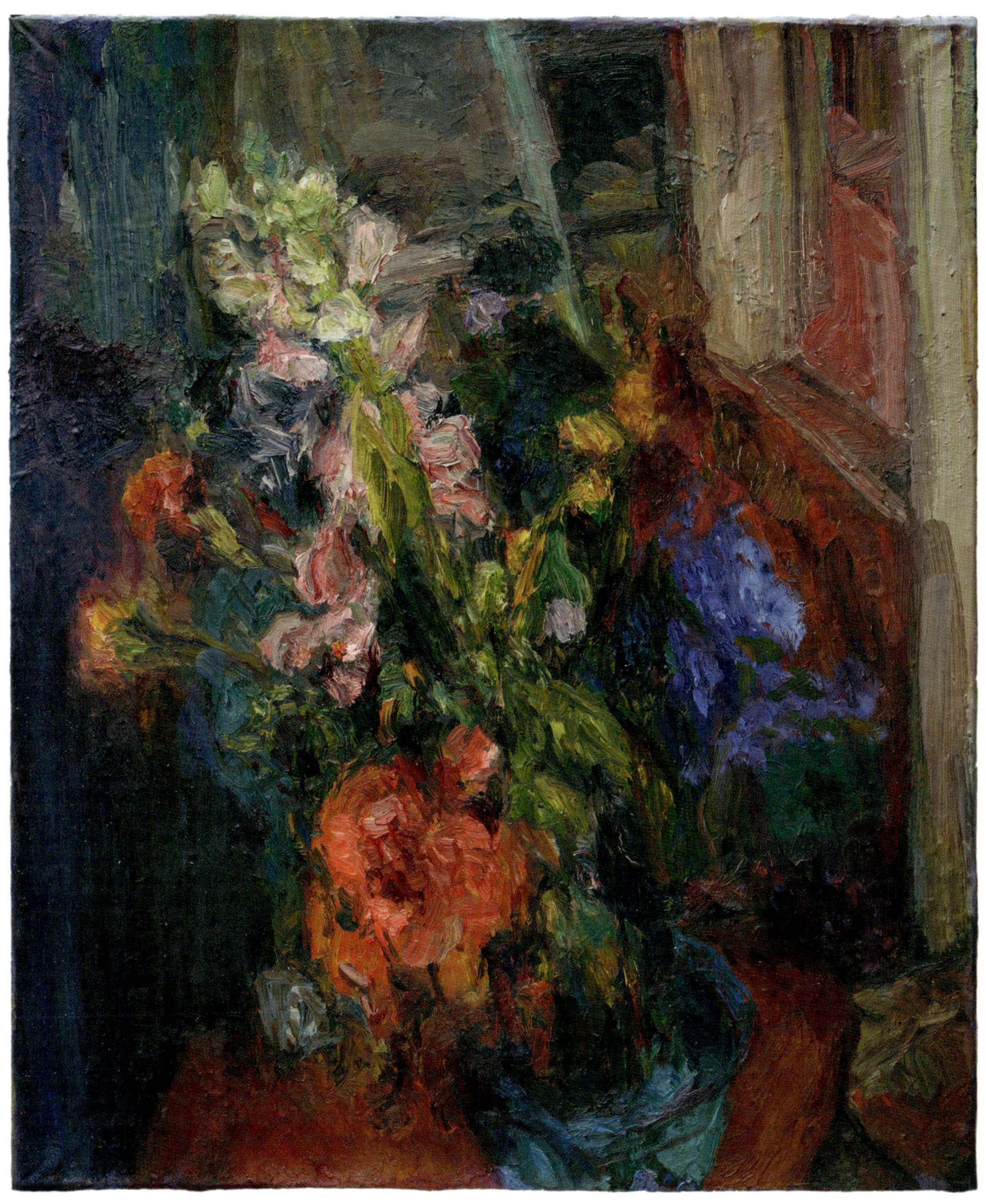

Andrew Cranston

Born 1969

Animated marks of pink, green and yellow describe an abundant bouquet in Andrew Cranston's *Misshapes*. The shapes of roses, daffodils and leaves are suggested only by a few lines. The explosion of flowers balancing on the table illuminates the room. In the background, cast in shadows, is an expressionless figure, who looks on at the blooms from afar. In the foreground, a number of objects, including a bright white wheel of brie, reflect the title of the work. *Misshapes* depicts a private, dreamlike world, which slowly reveals itself to the viewer.

Approaching painting like a storyteller, Cranston merges the ordinary and extraordinary, memory and fiction. Édouard Vuillard, Pierre Bonnard and Henri Matisse's depictions of the everyday rituals within the home are key points of reference for the artist. Cranston's work is placed firmly within the domestic realm. Painting on old linen book covers, he exposes the world of the text visually, subverting the function of the original material. His process involves an assiduous layering of paint, lacquer, bleach, varnish and collage, as well as long periods of time away from his compositions, creating a strange sense of intimacy whereby the stories that unfold in the paintings remain indefinite and uncanny.

The thickly applied paint and varnish in *Misshapes* gives the work an enamelled appearance. The poet Théophile Gautier described the work of the nineteenth-century enamel painter Claudius Popelin as being 'like a flower in amber', due to the medium's resistance to fading. Cranston's layered process gives a feeling of permanence to an otherwise temporary or fleeting moment, the spectral haze around the flowers perhaps shielding them from the figure who might move or discard them. *MB*

Misshapes, 2018
Oil and varnish on hardback book cover
26 x 19.5 cm
Courtesy the artist and Ingleby Gallery

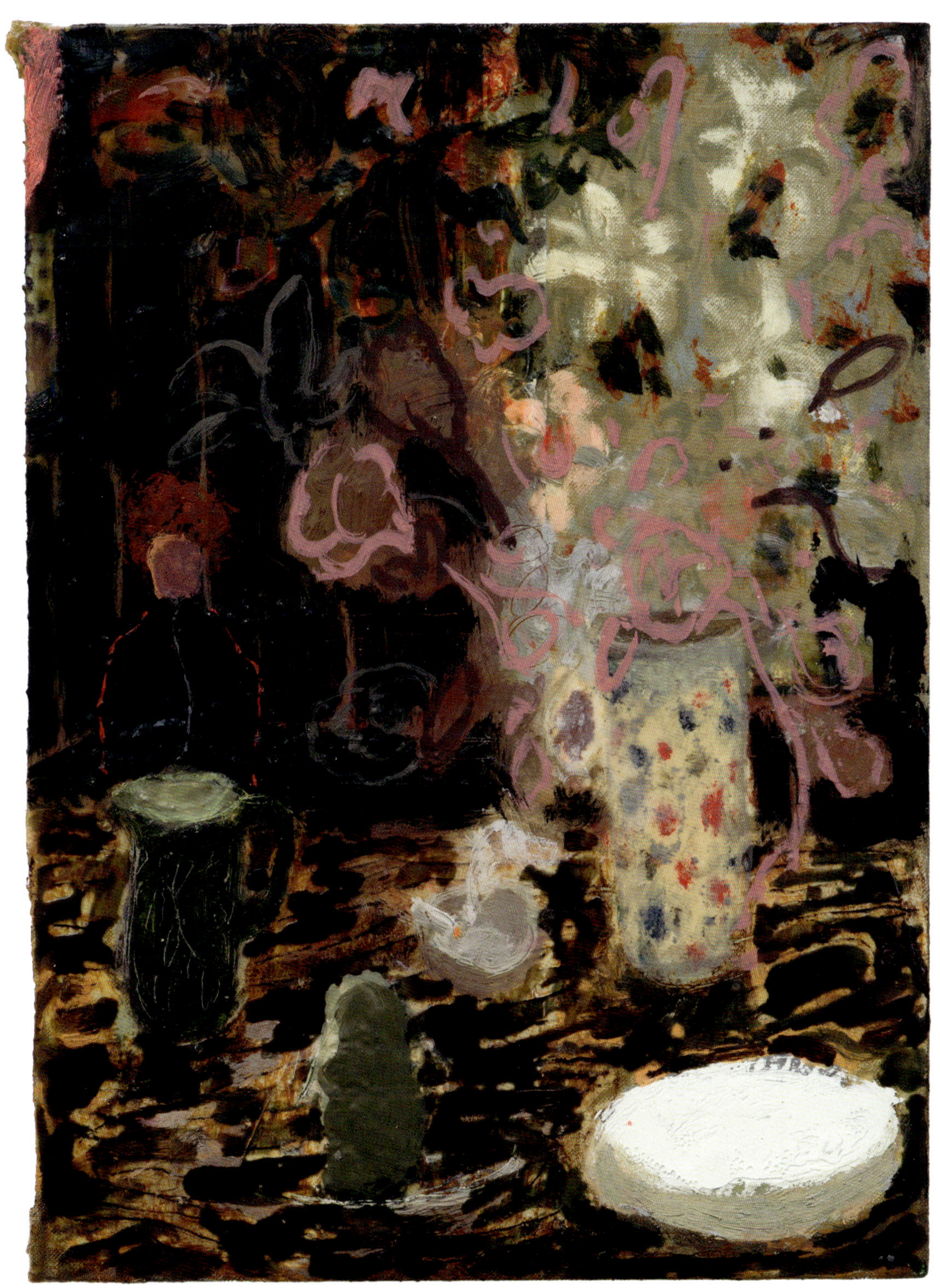

Kaye Donachie

Born 1970

A ghostly face looms over two picked roses in Kaye Donachie's *Monument to Every Moment*. While the painting has a melancholic palette of blue and green, the face is described in soft grey hues, as though interpolated from a black-and-white photograph. With this tonal contrast, our eyes are drawn to the romantic roses in the foreground, conjured from just a few loose, light brush marks.

Donachie is known for her close-up, cinematic paintings of women, inspired by figures of the twentieth-century avant-garde. Drawing on the work of artists and writers like Nina Hamnett, Lee Miller and Iris Tree, Donachie devises compositions that explore the aesthetic and emotional lives of these women, without aiming to recreate their likenesses. Her paintings of faces are not portraits, but evocations of a mood, moment or feeling. Flowers appear occasionally in Donachie's work, either alongside a face or hand, or as the main subject. In *Roses Slumber* (2024), vibrant blooms are set against a pastel-coloured sunset. In *We Together* (2018), a bunch of white flowers stands in a vase, while an abstract line darts and dances around it. There is the sense that Donachie is luxuriating in the effects of the paint itself. She has said: 'I enjoy the visceral qualities of paint and the evocative painterly marks that can facilitate our emotional connections to an image.'

While creating *Monument to Every Moment*, Donachie was researching the work of Mary Potter (1900-81), an artist known for her muted, enigmatic paintings. The bluish tint in the painting may refer to Potter's seaside home and studio in Aldeburgh, on the coast of Suffolk. The title juxtaposes the permanent ('monument') and the fleeting ('moment'), a temporal confrontation that is particularly resonant in paintings which crystallise the short lifespan of a flower. *NP*

Monument to Every Moment, 2026
Oil on linen
51 x 35.5 cm
Courtesy the artist and
Maureen Paley, London

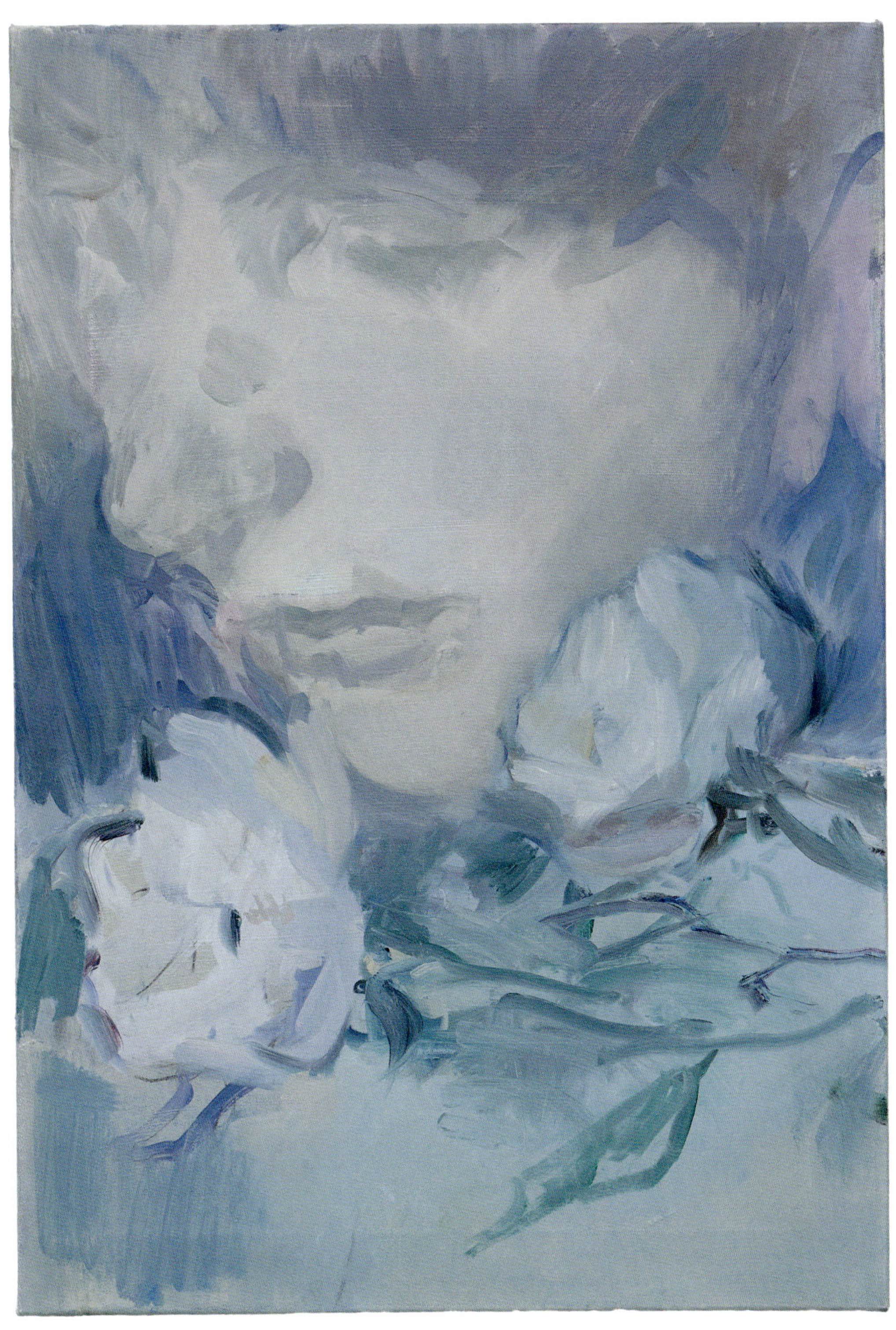

Gigi Ettedgui

Born 1992

A sprig of blossom in a household jar is the subject of Gigi Ettedgui's flower painting. The artist uses lead-white paint, known for its luminous appearance, to depict the milky petals. Set against a dark background, they have a glowing radiance. Primarily working in portraiture, Ettedgui gives flowers the same importance as she would a human subject. 'I think of my flowers as portraits', she has said. Unlike her paintings of people, however, which are sometimes created over the course of several months, her floral pieces are always made in a single day.

Ettedgui made this painting in the springtime, during the short period in which blossoms are in full bloom. She picked the sprig during a dog walk and took it to her studio where she painted it from life in natural lighting. Ettedgui trained in the 'sight-size method', a classical technique where artists position themselves at a fixed viewpoint, placing the canvas next to the subject to compare shapes and proportions. Created from direct observation, the painting represents the flowers with a high degree of accuracy. The obscured backdrop, which takes the composition out of its real-life context, elevates the simple blossom sprig to an archetypal status.

Many of Ettedgui's flower paintings are titled with the date of their making, referencing the short timeframe in which they are created. This painting's title alludes to the three petals that have fallen from the blossom. Ettedgui deliberately captured the moment at which the flower began to shed its petals. She sees the act of painting as a way of suspending time and defying the natural ephemerality of a flower's lifespan. Though the blossoms are now long dead, the painting that documents their aliveness lives on. ***NP***

As It Falls, 2025
Oil on canvas
50 x 40 cm
Courtesy the artist

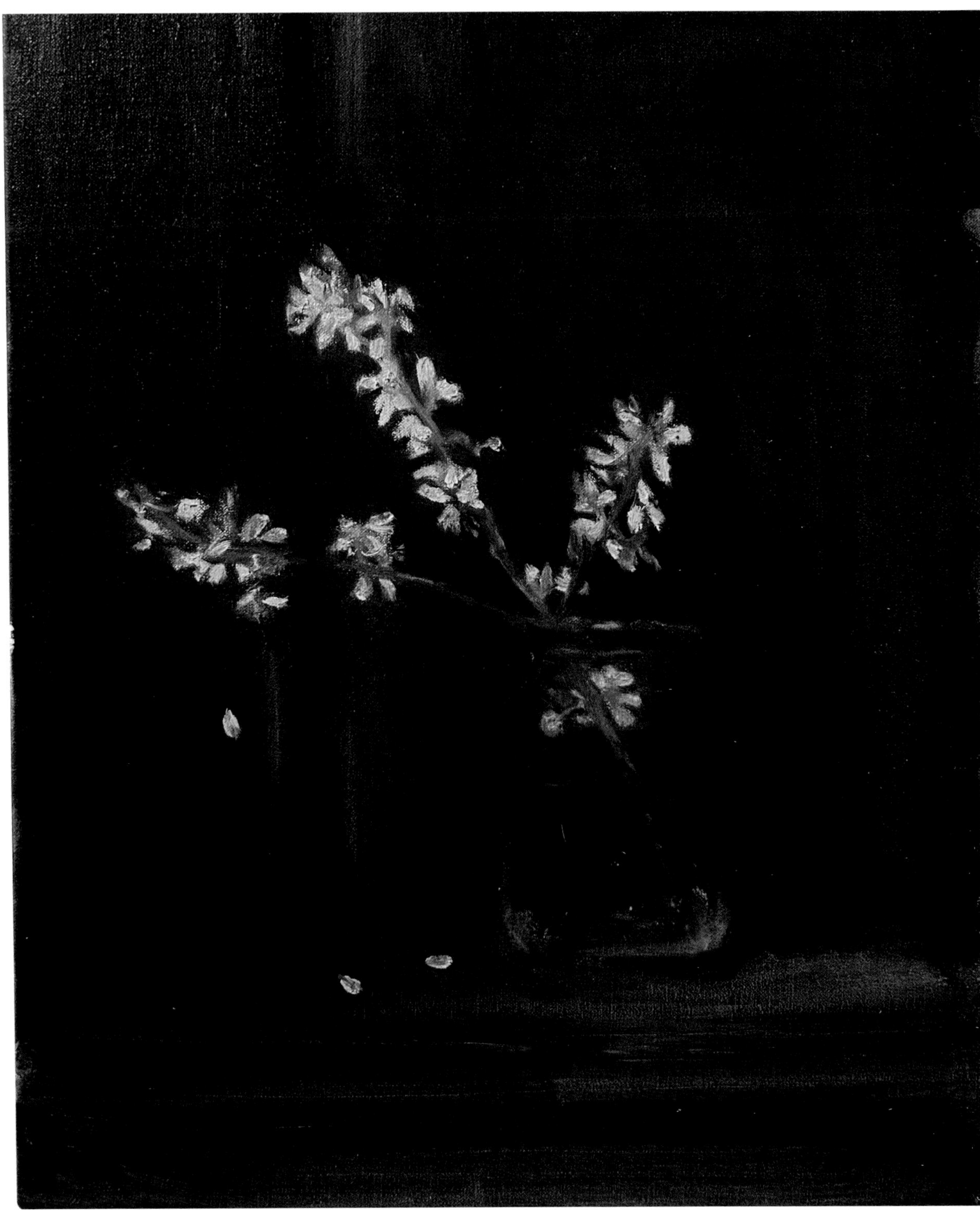

Anna Freeman Bentley

Born 1982

An intricate play of light and shadow animates Anna Freeman Bentley's painting of a vase of flowers. The window in the foreground, reflected in the glass vase and on the chest of drawers, floods the scene with light. The flowers seem to have their own luminescence, their pinkness transferred onto various surfaces around them. The wall behind, however, is cast in shadows, as is the room glimpsed in the background. The grey tones and angular lines of the architectural space emphasise the softness of the organic objects: the voluptuous flowers, unruly leaves and taut red berries.

Freeman Bentley always begins her artistic process with photographs, in this case taken in Helen Ede's bedroom in the Kettle's Yard house. The painting's title has several possible referents: the arrangement of flowers, the arrangement of the domestic space, or Freeman Bentley's arrangement of the composition. The artist subtly manipulated the configuration of the room in her painting, bringing in more of the surrounding interior and enlarging the flowers.

Throughout her artistic career Freeman Bentley has depicted places charged with invisible meaning and purpose. Her interiors are unpeopled, but not unoccupied: she seeks out spaces that are layered with history. Kettle's Yard, once a home, has special resonance in this context. In Freeman Bentley's painting the real space of the bedroom becomes transformed and reimagined. The objects on the table and windowsill – a starfish, pomander and geode – are made strange and alien by the oversized blooms. The flowers themselves, emerging from washy brushstrokes of loose paint, take on a symbolic quality, connecting the present with a past that can only really be guessed at. ***NP***

Arrangement III, 2025
Oil on panel
60 x 50 cm
Courtesy the artist

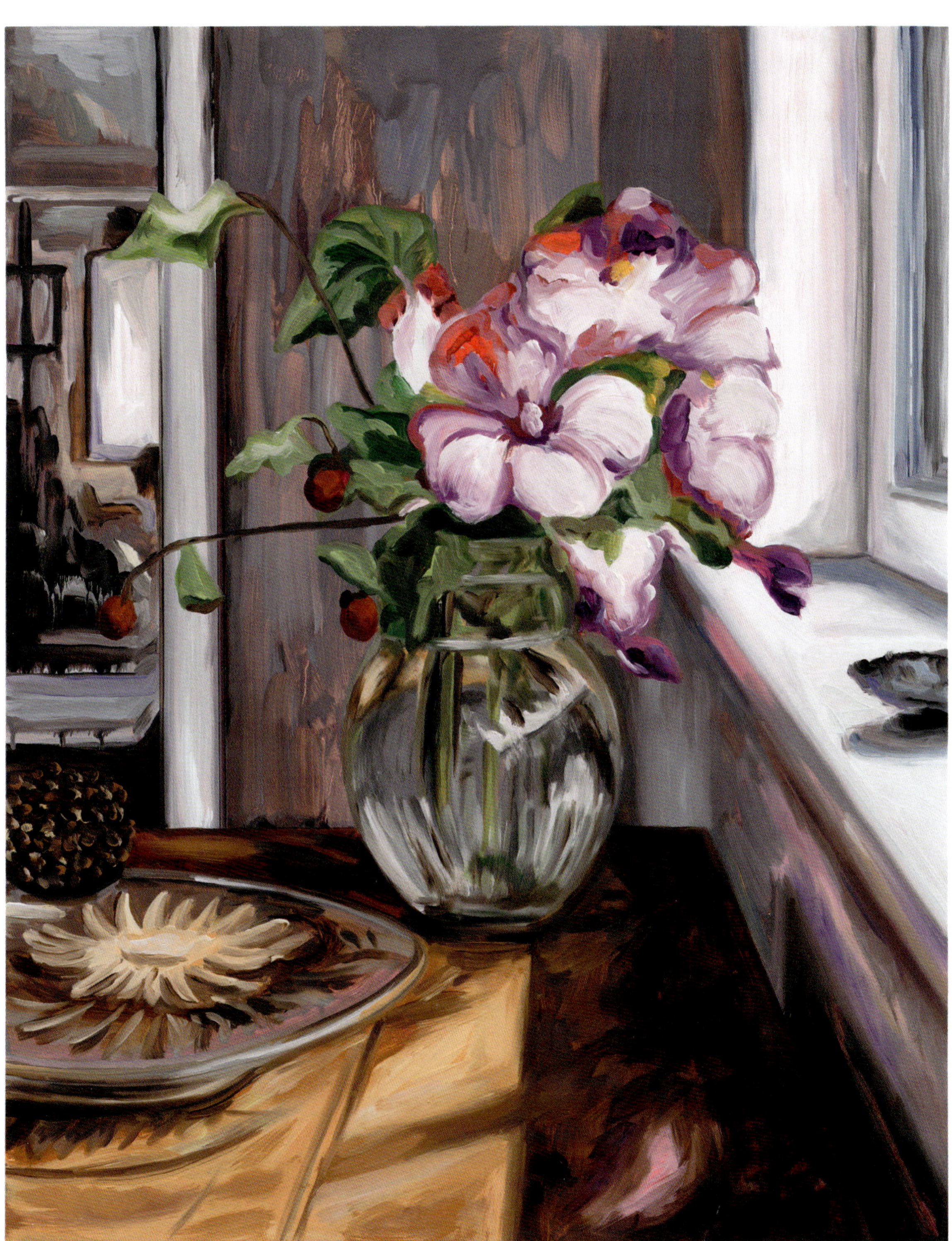

Marjory Garnett

1897–1977

Three types of Arctic flower are depicted in Marjory Garnett's delicate watercolour: golden yellow saxifrage, ivory-white poppies and cup-shaped cassiope. The painting is from a sketchbook containing 14 watercolours made by Garnett during a cruise to the Norwegian island of Spitsbergen in 1930. Partly created in situ, the painting includes pencil-written 'notes to self' about the scale and identification of the flowers. Of the saxifrage and poppies, she writes 'about 1/1' and of the cassiope 'very slightly enlarged', showing her aim to represent the flowers at life-size. She deliberates over the identification of the flowers: she crosses out 'St John's Wort' and replaces it with 'Saxifraga Hirculus'; ponders 'Heath?' before concluding 'Cassiope'.

The watercolour was created primarily for a scientific purpose, documenting plant species that are native to the region. The Arctic poppy has subsequently been identified by researchers from the Scott Polar Research Institute in Cambridge as the most northerly flowering plant in the world. However, Garnett's creative intentions are evident too. As well as her works made on expeditions, she created luscious oil paintings of flowers set in domestic interiors. In her watercolours, she observes minute details and deftly translates them onto the page.

The flowers in this painting echo and reflect one another in an elegant play of correspondences. The pair of dangling cassiope heads are mirrored in the larger drooping poppies, while the sprawling bed of foliage on the poppy plant is reflected, in different ways, by the tangle of leaves on the saxifrage and the shrubby end of the cassiope. Garnett also captures the distinctive colours and textures of the plants: the papery poppies on their furry stalks, the orange-red spots on the saxifrage petals and the wiry red pedicels holding up the bell-like cassiope. Some pencil outlines are left unpainted, showing how the plants come to life through Garnett's application of paint. *NP*

Advent Bay, Spitsbergen, Assorted Flora, 1930
Watercolour on paper
28.8 x 19.5 cm
Lent by the Polar Museum, Scott Polar Research Institute, University of Cambridge

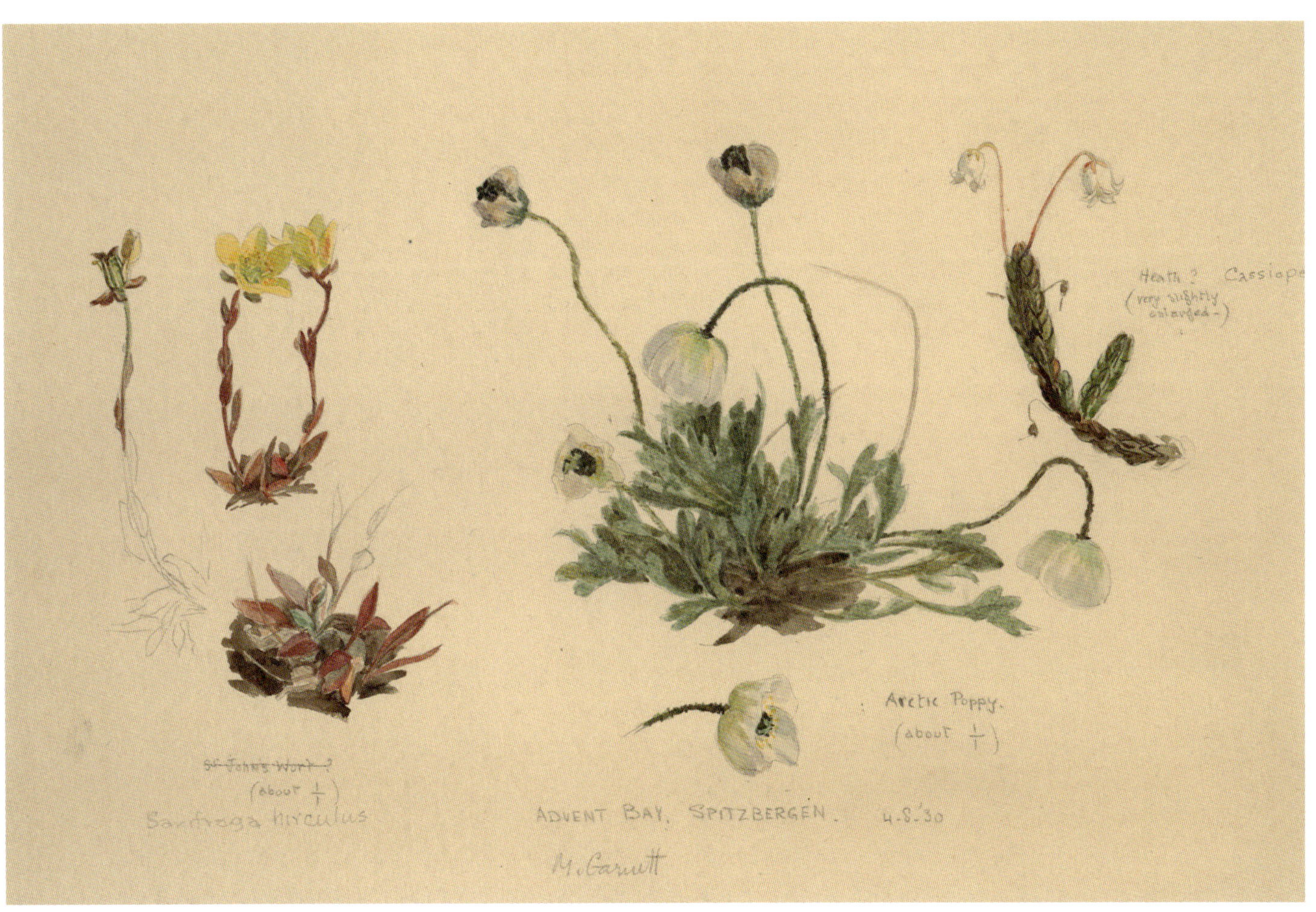

Heath ? Cassiope
(very slightly enlarged -)
Arctic Poppy.
(about 1/1)
St Johns Wort ?
(about 1/1)
Saxifraga hirculus
ADVENT BAY, SPITZBERGEN. 4.8.30
M. Garnett

Tirzah Garwood

1908–1950

Above a cluster of wildflowers swaying in the breeze hovers a small, model-like aeroplane in Tirzah Garwood's *Springtime of Flight*. The sky is partly calm and blue, partly turbulent and overcast, giving the composition a subtle sense of threat. The flight of the aeroplane is mirrored by that of the large butterfly. With its butter-yellow colour, it stands out against the landscape behind, as do the jewel-like tulips, daffodils and daisies. This painting is one of 20 small works that Garwood created in the last year of her life after being diagnosed with cancer in 1948. Her depictions of flowers allude to small moments of happiness at a time when she was often confined to bed and in pain.

Garwood trained and worked as a wood engraver but was prolific in various artistic mediums, producing oil paintings, watercolours, embroidery, marbelled papers and three-dimensional models. Although attuned to modern art movements through her artist friends Paul Nash and Peggy Angus, and her marriage to artist Eric Ravilious, she was also influenced by botanical drawing techniques and Victorian children's book illustrations. Her multitude of references, both historic and contemporary, accumulated into the creation of surreal, dreamlike worlds.

Springtime of Flight conveys the anxieties of Garwood's life. In 1942 Ravilious was reported missing-in-action following an air rescue mission off the coast of Iceland, leaving Garwood to care for their three young children. The aeroplane in Garwood's painting, which appears small and fragile against the menacing sky, may be a reference to her husband's tragic death. Garwood's own heightened sense of mortality might be captured by the singular daffodil, the most wilted of the flowers, which resembles the butterfly in size and colour. Symbols of springtime and new life, daffodils and butterflies are also known for their temporality. In Garwood's painting, their poignant meaning becomes apparent. *MB*

Springtime of Flight, 1950
Oil on canvas
30.5 x 40.5 cm
Private collection

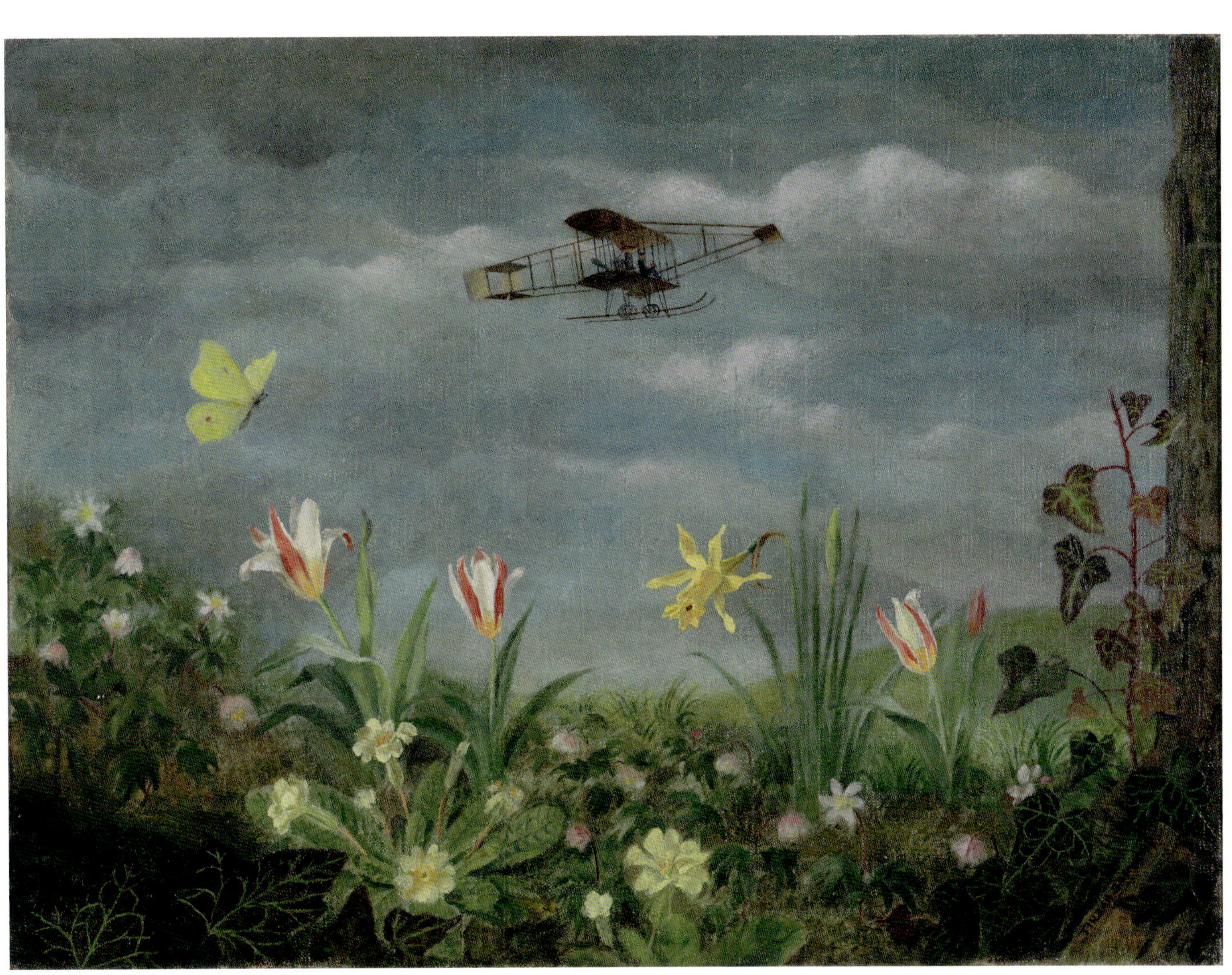

Gluck
1895–1978

An arrangement of convolvulus cascades out of an immaculate glass in Gluck's painting, the stems curling up and down in graceful arabesques. The white trumpet-shaped flowers are in a state of perfect bloom. Convolvulus wilts in just a few hours, so Gluck had to forage in the garden hedgerows for replacement flowers from which to paint. It took five weeks of constant work for her to complete this painting.

Gluck began to paint flowers in 1932 when she was introduced to the celebrity florist, Constance Spry. Their mutual friend, interior designer Prudence Maufe, ordered a bunch of white blooms from Spry for Gluck's new studio. Spry sent a bouquet of convolvulus which Gluck thought so beautiful that she was inspired to paint it. When Spry and Gluck then met, they fell instantly in love. Their romance ended four years later when Gluck left Spry for the socialite Nesta Obermer. *Convolvulus* was painted in 1940, while Gluck was lodging with Obermer in her East Sussex home, taking refuge from wartime London. In the months before, Gluck had suffered from a serious depressive episode, partly prompted by Obermer's refusal to separate from her husband. With this choice of subject, so intimately connected to her relationship with Spry, Gluck may have intended to elicit sexual jealousy in Obermer.

Though a common weed, the convolvulus in Gluck's painting is exquisite and enticing. The work has echoes of eighteenth-century Dutch still-life painting, a genre which was historically seen as the preserve of women artists. Gluck, however, did not feel that she belonged to this group. Born Hannah Gluckstein, she adopted the genderless mononym 'Gluck' and throughout her life dressed in masculine clothing. For Gluck, flowers were expressions of love and eroticism outside of gender. Of her floral painting *Lords and Ladies*, she wrote, suggestively: 'I feel like a bee ... penetrating them for their sweetness.' ***NP***

Convolvulus, 1940
Oil on canvas
40.2 x 32.4 cm
Private collection, courtesy of
The Fine Art Society Ltd

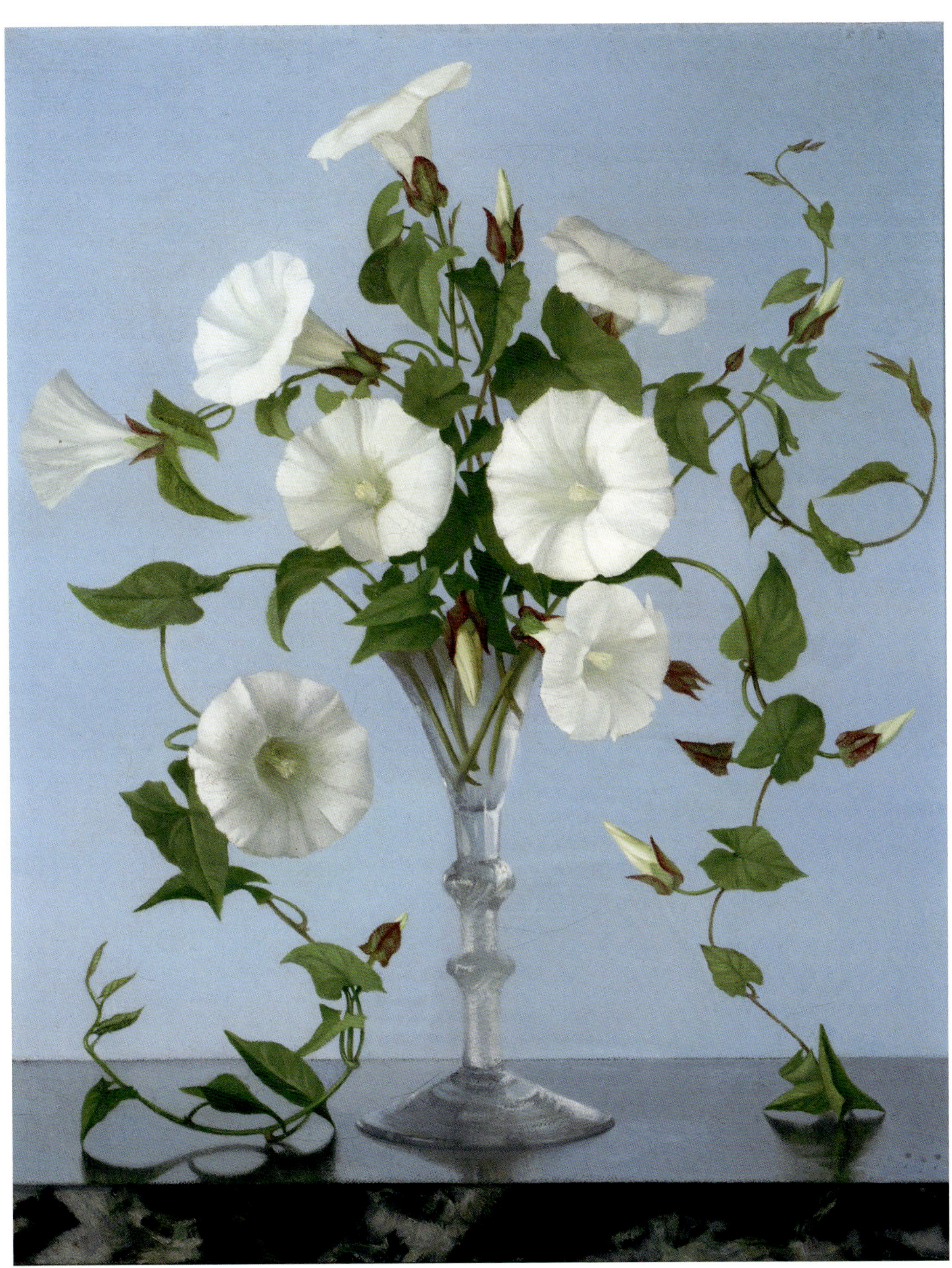

Lubaina Himid

Born 1954

Forget-me-nots, peonies, dahlias, tulips, palm leaves and many other flowers appear in a kaleidoscopic array in Lubaina Himid's painting *These Are For You*. The display of flowers, contained within psychedelic forms, spills out of the square composition and onto the painted frame. The border itself is painted a leaf-like green and features decorative details on each of its four corners, which draw out colours from the main composition. Arranged like a patchwork of mementoes, the flowers are like a secret language for the viewer to decipher and translate.

Like in many of Himid's works, there is a balance between the regularity of the pattern and the originality of each form. Floral motifs recur throughout her work, including her large-scale paintings, installations, prints, textiles and ceramics. Human figures feature prominently in her paintings, but her visual language is also informed by organic forms and colours. Himid's compositions are often inspired by her collection of East African *kangas* – fabrics with a large decorative border and a central motif painted in vivid colours, a format echoed in this painting.

Human presence is often conveyed in Himid's work, whether or not a figure is present, through the inclusion of *trompe l'oeil* stitching or the depiction of domestic objects. Here the human presence is implied through the patchwork of floral motifs, which resemble fabric swatches presented for the viewer to peruse. Many of Himid's works feature conversations between people and in this painting she creates a dialogue with the viewer. *These Are For You* suggests a display of the artist's archive of references. The title acts as an invitation for the viewer to observe and explore the flowers, not only their personal significance but also their historical and cultural connotations. *MB*

These Are For You, 2025
Acrylic on canvas
28 x 28 cm
Courtesy the artist,
Hollybush Gardens, London and
Greene Naftali, New York

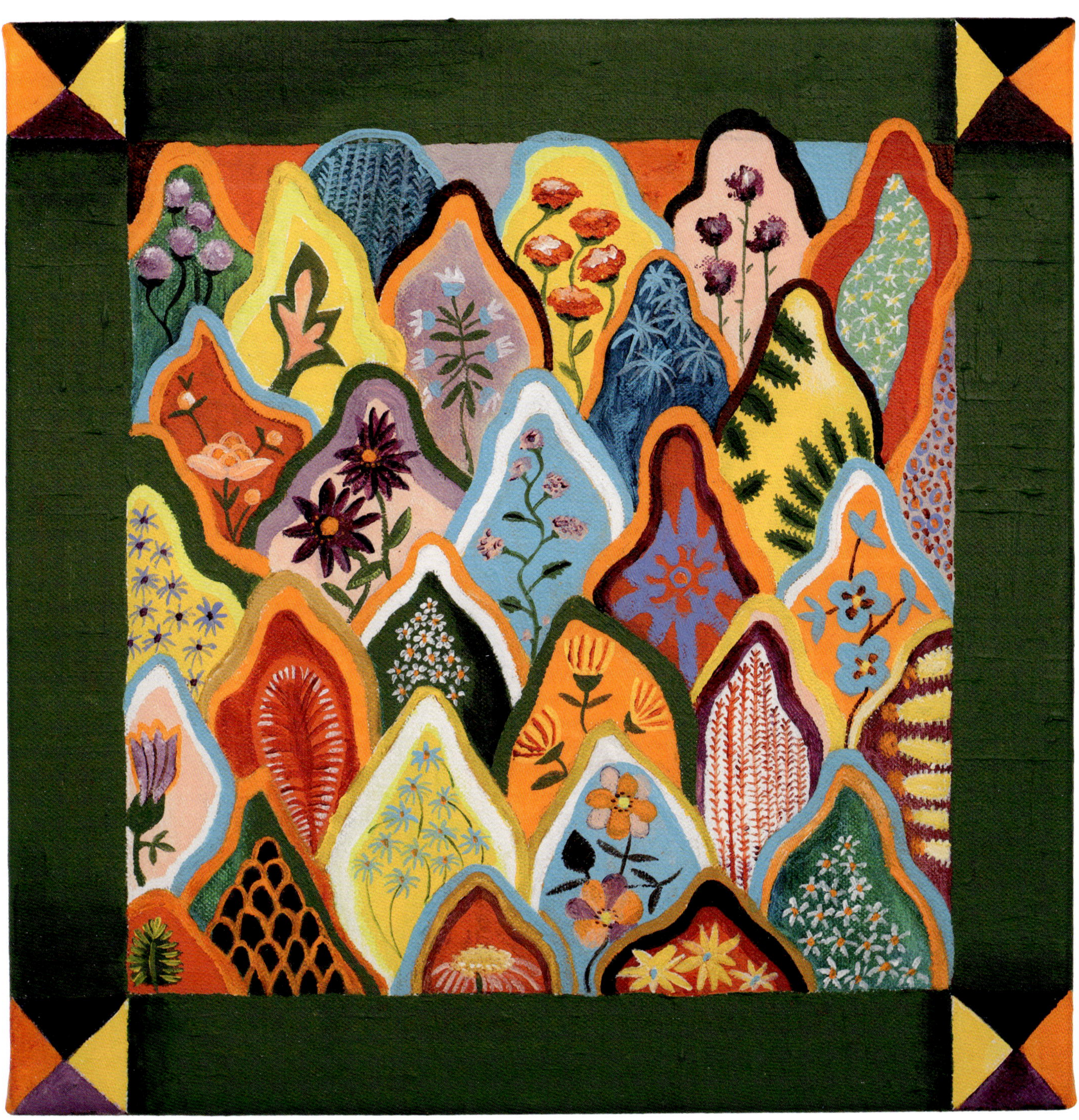

Howard Hodgkin

1932–2017

Howard Hodgkin's 'red flowers' are conjured from dramatic stripes of red and green paint. The brushstrokes sweep across the wooden surface, with no clear beginning or end, continuing past the edge of the painting and its frame. The red and green colours overlap and intermingle, becoming diffuse in some areas and coalescing in others. They also interact with the brown and white paint marks that trace the shape of the frame. Against the grain of the wood, some of which is left exposed, the paint looks glossy and beguiling.

Hodgkin's paintings often refer to personal memories and experiences. This work was inspired by Hodgkin's father, Eliot, who was a passionate gardener and plant collector. Hodgkin said of the painting: 'My father loved small flowers – I was thinking about him.' The smallness of the flowers is reflected in the scale of the painting, which is not much bigger than a posy. The flowers that are depicted, however, are magnified and expanded to a representation of pure colour. Early in his artistic career, Hodgkin began exclusively painting on wooden board. Here its quality as an organic material is made evident, creating a harmony between the medium and subject matter.

Hodgkin was conscious of the role that flowers play in matters of life and death. In 1990 he created a print titled *The Hospital Room was Choked with Flowers, Everybody Likes Flowers, Surplus Flowers, the Room was Filling up with Flowers* to accompany a short story by Susan Sontag about the death of an unnamed man from AIDS. In *Red Flowers* Hodgkin evokes his father, who had died almost 40 years before. Though Hodgkin's titles refer to specific places, events and objects, his works are never illustrative. Instead, they communicate moments, emotions and intense, all-encompassing sensory experiences. ***NP***

Red Flowers, 2011–12
Oil on wood
21.3 x 23.5 cm
Private collection, London

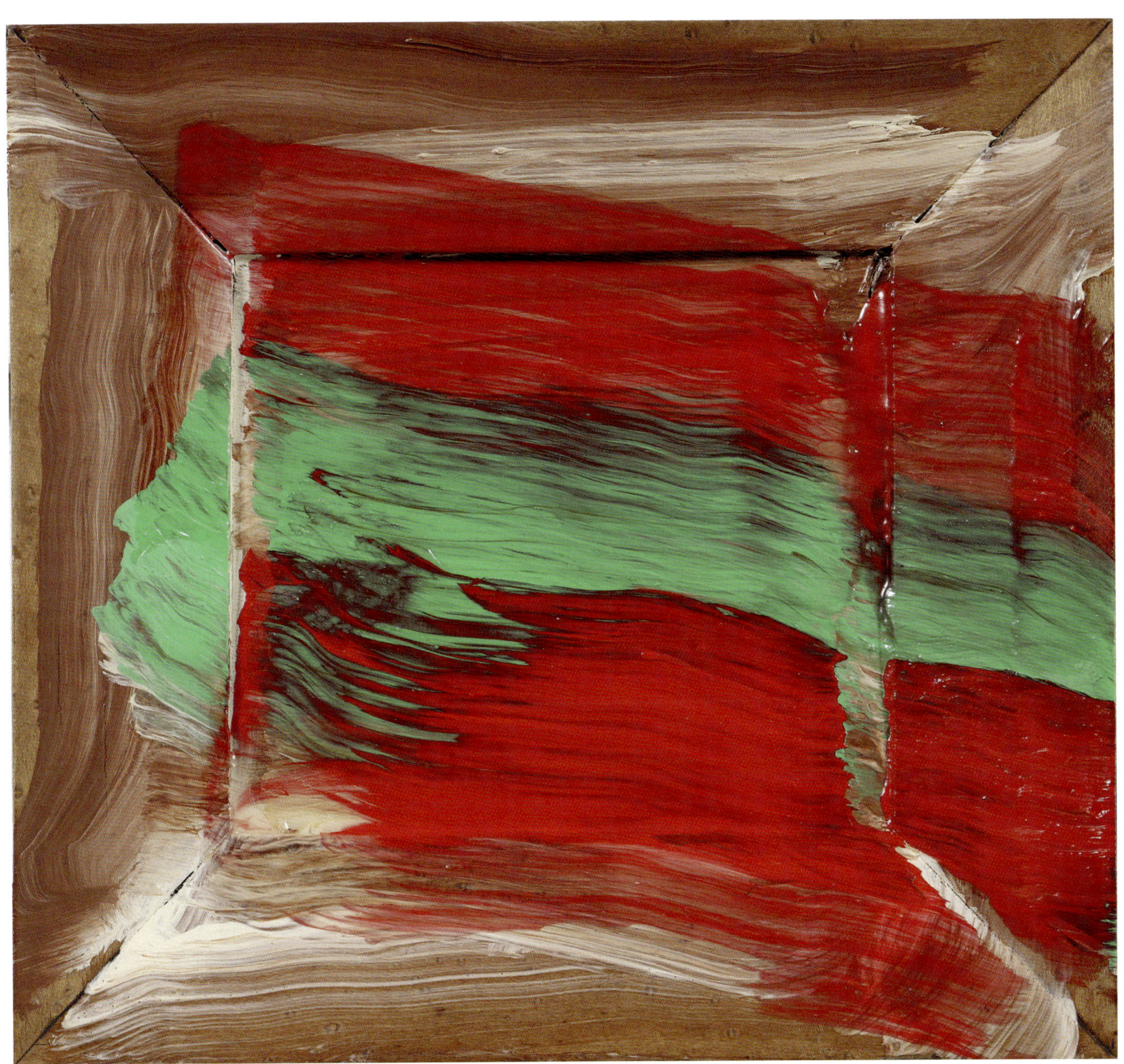

Isak of Igdlorpait

1866–1903

Six colourful drawings of flowers and seedpods appear in the sketchbook of Isak of Igdlorpait. This small selection of studies represents the natural forms through bold lines and colours, suggesting the artist's knowledge of his subject. Each drawing is annotated in Kalaallisut (Greenlandic), however Isak's script has later been translated into Danish by another hand: above his sketch reads: 'Flowers that look like a man's heart!!'.

Having lost his right arm in a hunting accident, Isak worked as a shepherd for the Moravian missionaries in their Igdlorpait outpost in southwest Greenland. As payment for his work, he received paper and paints, enabling him to document life in the settlement. This sketchbook is one of three known to exist by Isak of Igdlorpait. His depictions of everyday life at the turn of the twentieth century in Greenland provide insightful historical records. Isak's work built on the arrival of print culture in Greenland during the 1860s, as well as on a much longer tradition of natural history supported by the missions.

Throughout the pages of the sketchbook, Isak depicts scenes of local life featuring boats, fish and other animals, the surrounding landscape and buildings. The flowers appear towards the end, opposite a drawing of the artist's own tools: a sketchbook and pen. As a subject of colonial rule, Isak's use of European materials and artistic methods is somewhat counteracted by his depictions of indigenous Greenlandic costumes, structures and ways of life. The means of documenting his experiences of the world and community around him, including the flora and fauna of the Arctic, accumulates into a record of an artist at one with his surroundings and observant of the environment around him. *MB*

Sketchbook, circa 1900
Watercolour and ink on paper
21.5 x 17.2 cm
Lent by the Polar Museum,
Scott Polar Research Institute,
University of Cambridge

En Bog og en Pen.

atuagkat aglågtålo.

Blomster som ligne et Menneskehjerte!!

umalåla
paussut isup åssinga.

Nerys Johnson
1942–2001

A honeysuckle and two rosehips are brought to life in magenta pink and fiery orange in Nerys Johnson's small but animated watercolour painting. The plants are set against a monochrome black background, which intensifies their vibrancy. The description of the honeysuckle in the painting's title as 'looking right' confers a sense of agency and vitality on the flower. Viewers of the painting are placed in a position of mimicking the subject's own act of looking, creating an intimacy between the two.

Johnson made this work several months before she died at the age of 58. From early childhood the artist lived with rheumatoid arthritis, a condition that affected both her working method and subject matter. For much of her artistic life she based herself in a studio in the front room of her home in Durham. She painted while seated in a mechanised chair and used a long wooden pole as an aid. Cut flowers, easily available and endlessly varied, were an ideal subject for her improvised circumstances. She painted mostly with watercolour and gouache, mediums that can be revisited and adapted, allowing for periods of forced rest.

By the late 1990s, Johnson's arthritis had evolved and she found it challenging to undertake even small tasks including preparing surfaces on which to paint. In the final two years of her life she enlisted her care assistants to tear fragments of paper on which she painted a sequence of brightly coloured watercolours, including this one. Each work is dated on the back with the specific day it was created, giving the series a diaristic quality. The brushstrokes in the paintings, both effortful and assured, are shaped by the specific choreography of Johnson's body and movements – a record of the artist's physical embodiment, as much as a representation of the flowers. ***NP***

Honeysuckle (looking right) with two rosehips, 2000
Watercolour on paper
19 x 10 cm
The Women's Art Collection,
Murray Edwards College

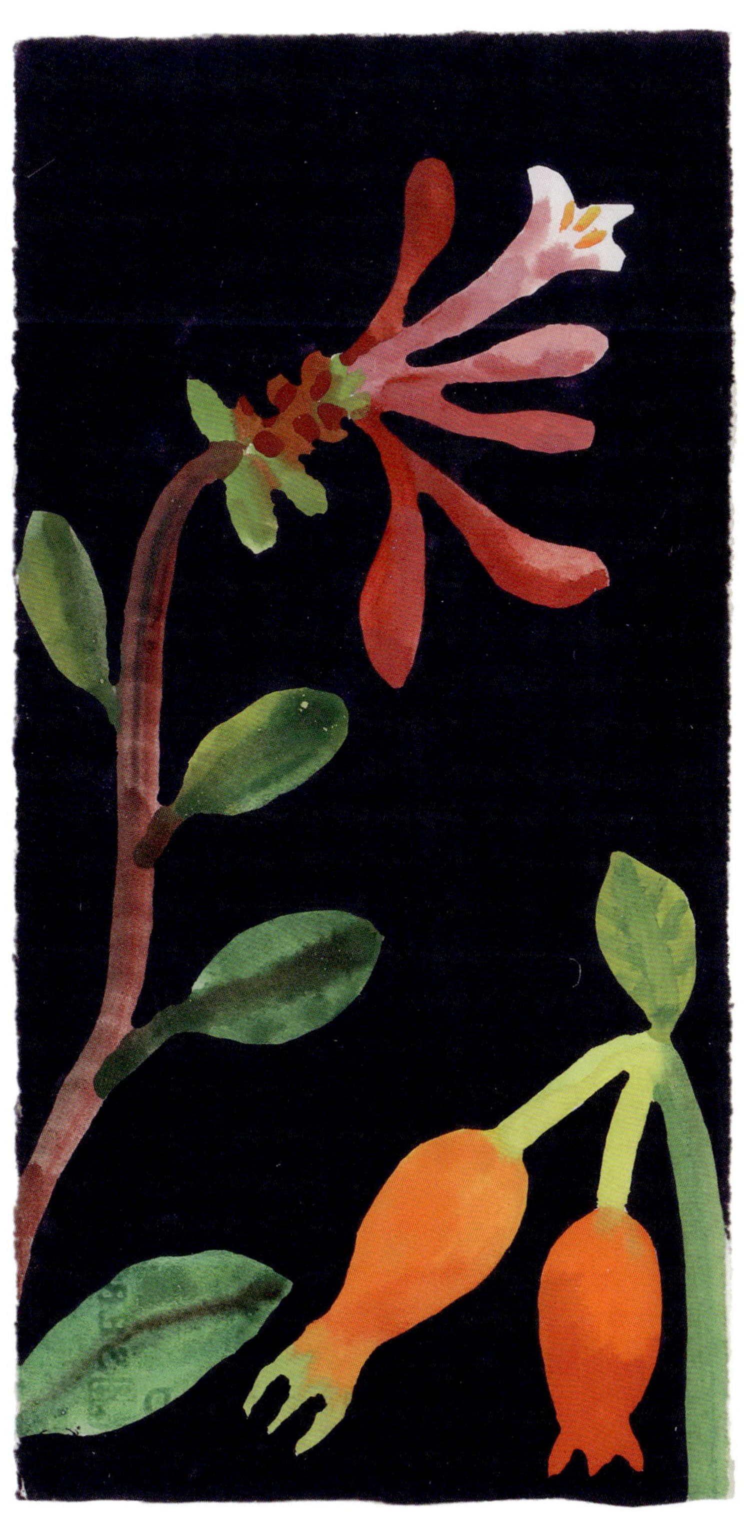

David Jones
1895–1974

Three sumptuous flower arrangements fill David Jones's layered composition. Each is contained in a different vessel and has its own distinct quality. The wispy, romantic bouquet in a metallic tankard is dominated by the oversized blue anemone that droops down towards the table. The small vase next to it holds a more colourful, varied array of flowers, while the large urn on the windowsill has an explosion of stems which are so lightly described that they almost completely recede into the background. In contrast with the overall washiness of the scene, certain floral details are rendered in bold, sharp pencil outlines and paint marks: the dense flower heads, thick leaf veins and black anemone centre.

Jones painted flowers throughout his life. This work was made during a period of intense creativity for the artist during which he shifted his focus away from meticulous engravings towards dreamlike watercolours. After serving on the Western Front during the First World War as a young man, Jones suffered from lifelong post-traumatic stress disorder and in October 1932 had the first of two major psychological breakdowns. The flower paintings he created after this were charged with deep symbolic meaning relating to his Catholic faith. However, his floral compositions of the late 1920s and early 1930s were more naturalistic, often created from direct observation and set within domestic interiors.

Like many of Jones's works, this watercolour was painted in front of a window with light filtering through. The impression of shimmering rays is created through the artist's application of pale, almost transparent colour. The walls, window, curtains and table all softly merge into one another so that the boundaries of the architectural space are hard to make out. Jones plays with the wateriness of his medium, engulfing his viewers within the flowing, flowering haze of the scene. *NP*

Untitled, circa 1930
Watercolour on paper
61.7 x 49 cm
Private collection

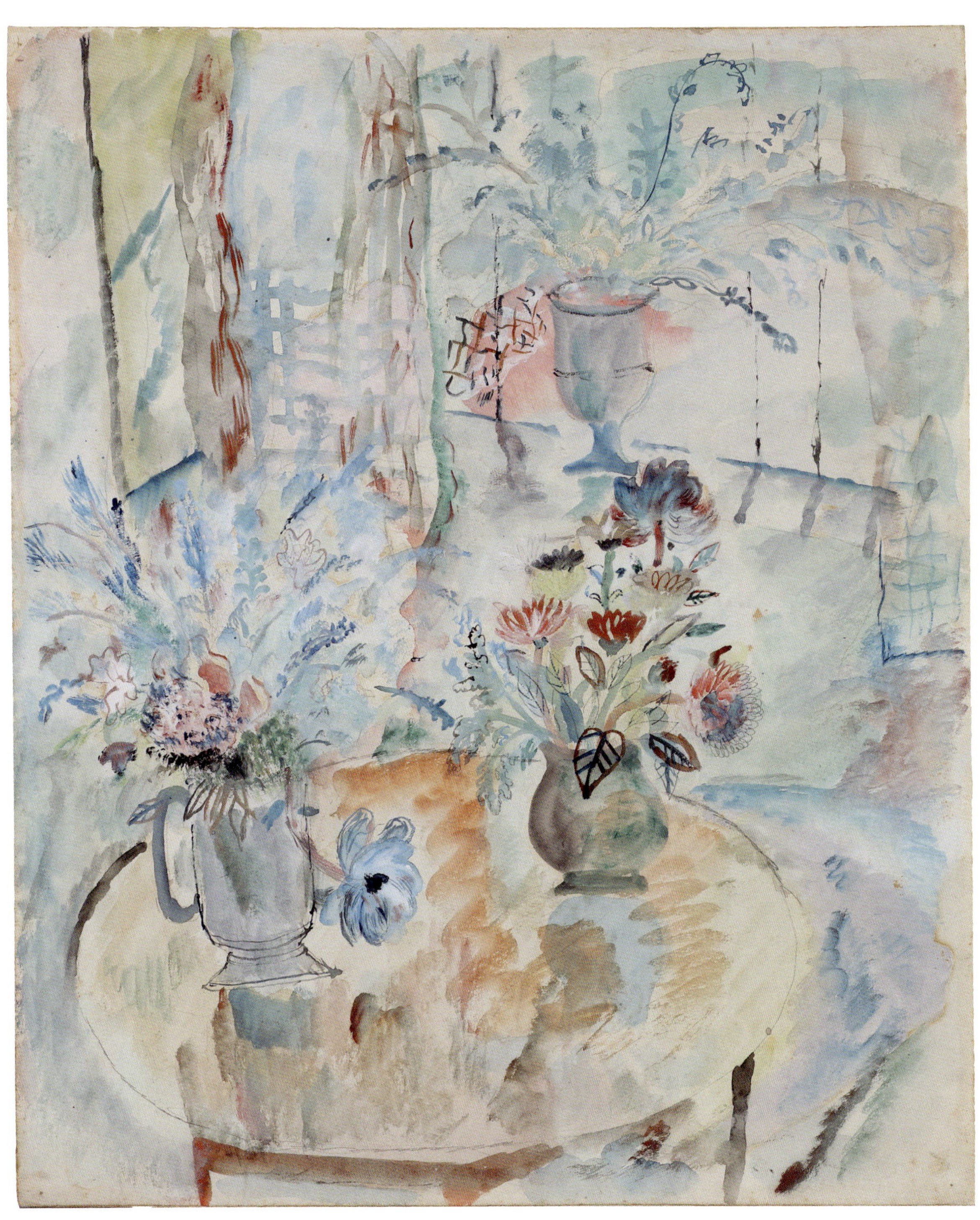

Poppy Jones

Born 1985

Illuminated against a moody cobalt blue background, a glistening glass vase contains a small assortment of flowers in Poppy Jones's *Still Spring*. The texture of the suede surface leaves the impression of the artist's fingerprints, the material taking on the appearance of a smooth smudged digital screen. This tactile effect encourages us to reflect on the dominant role of electronic devices in creating and disseminating images today. The use of suede also alludes to the surface of a mirror or window. Mimicking features of domestic architecture, *Still Spring* invites us to peer into a realm of stillness and light, removed from the distractions of the modern world.

Jones's layered process of making distils our experiences of both physical and digital reality. The artist captures images on her phone camera, which she then prints onto suede before painting parts of the composition in watercolour and ink. The colours become more saturated as the suede soaks up the paint, giving the work a magical quality, as if the image were emerging through the fabric itself. Jones refined this technique during the Covid-19 pandemic, when she began to make use of the subject matter and materials immediately available to her. She photographed her domestic surroundings and printed on found fabrics and old clothes.

Jones's approach to artmaking is strongly influenced by Modernist writings on the timeless realm inhabited by objects, for example the work of Gertrude Stein, Virginia Woolf and Alain Robbe-Grillet. The artist's paintings bring objects together in their own reality through glimpses of her domestic environment. The flowers are arrested in time, yet the ethereal quality of Jones's process and materials conveys the sense of their inevitable decay. ***MB***

Still Spring, 2022
Oil and watercolour on suede
29 x 21 cm
Private collection, London

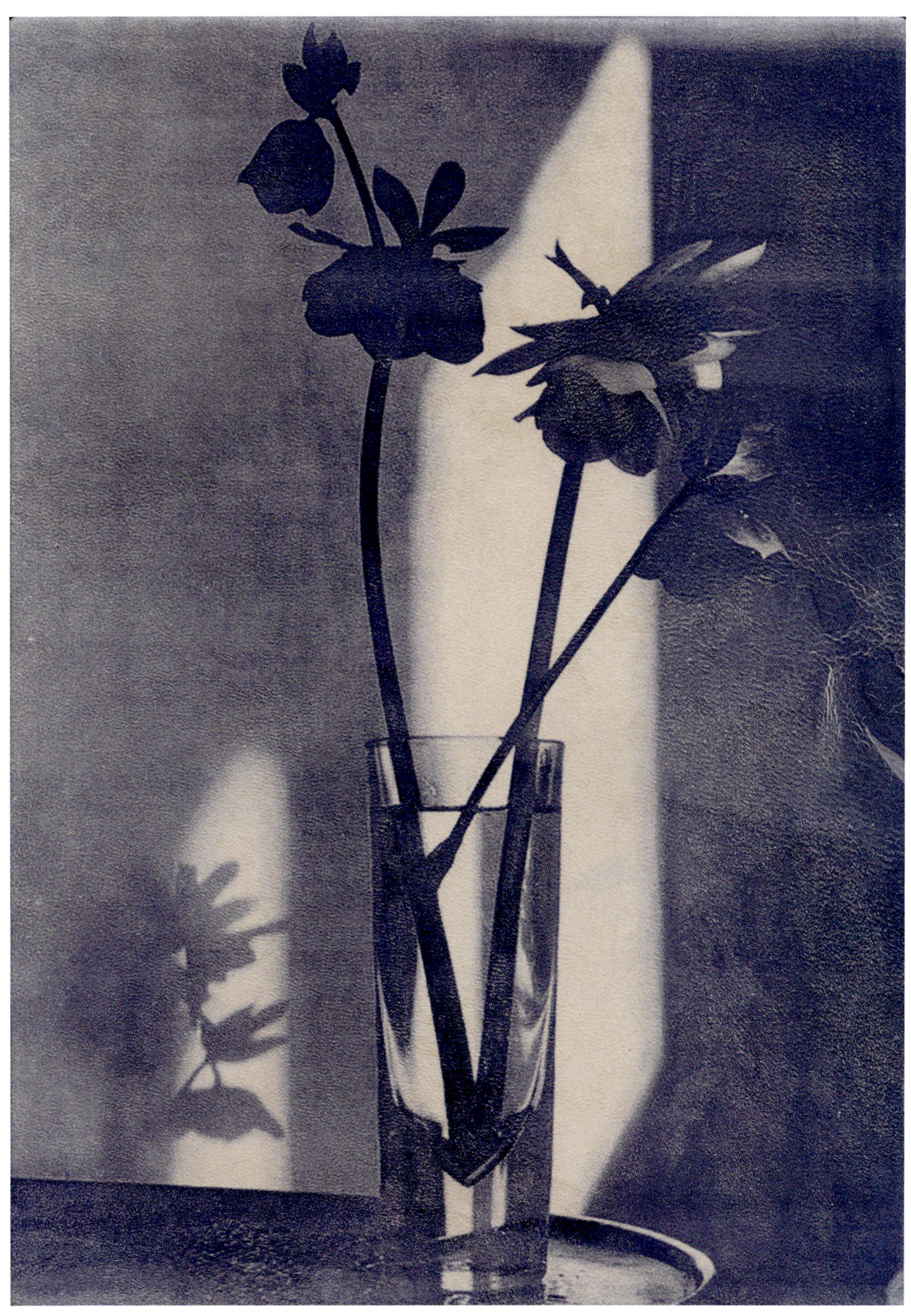

Joy Labinjo

Born 1994

A lush, abundant bouquet stands rigidly in a plain glass vase. The immaculate floral arrangement is composed of many different flowers and leaves: roses, lilacs, anemones, eucalyptus. The perfection of the bouquet, referenced in the painting's title, suggests that the plants are not based on real-life equivalents, but conjured from the artist's imagination.

This is one of three flower paintings which Joy Labinjo created as part of her series *Ode to Olaudah Equiano* (2022). Equiano was one of the leading figures of the British anti-slavery movement. His 1789 memoir, which recounts his experiences of enslavement, played a significant role in changing public opinion around abolition in Britain. Struck by the relative absence of historical records relating to Equiano's life, Labinjo created her series as a visual corrective. The paintings in her *Ode* include imagined portraits, scenes of Equiano's journey from Africa to England and depictions of his clothing and domestic objects. The three flower paintings point to the history of eighteenth-century still lifes as a display of wealth, often commissioned by those involved in the transatlantic slave trade. Within the context of this series, the tight binding around the flowers takes on a menacing meaning. The blooms are sumptuous but constrained. They have been removed from their natural context and made to perform a role as 'gift and centrepiece'.

Despite its historical inspiration, the painting has a strongly contemporary feel. Labinjo uses her distinctive painting style with its flat perspectives and sculpted forms. The classical black background is punctuated by an amorphous blue shape. The cylindrical glass vase, in which the stems are eerily magnified, resembles those sold in supermarkets. Everything in the painting is double-edged: old and new, cheap and expensive, beautiful and sinister. ***NP***

Perfect by Nature for Gift and Centrepiece, 2022
Oil on canvas
90 x 60 cm
Courtesy the artist

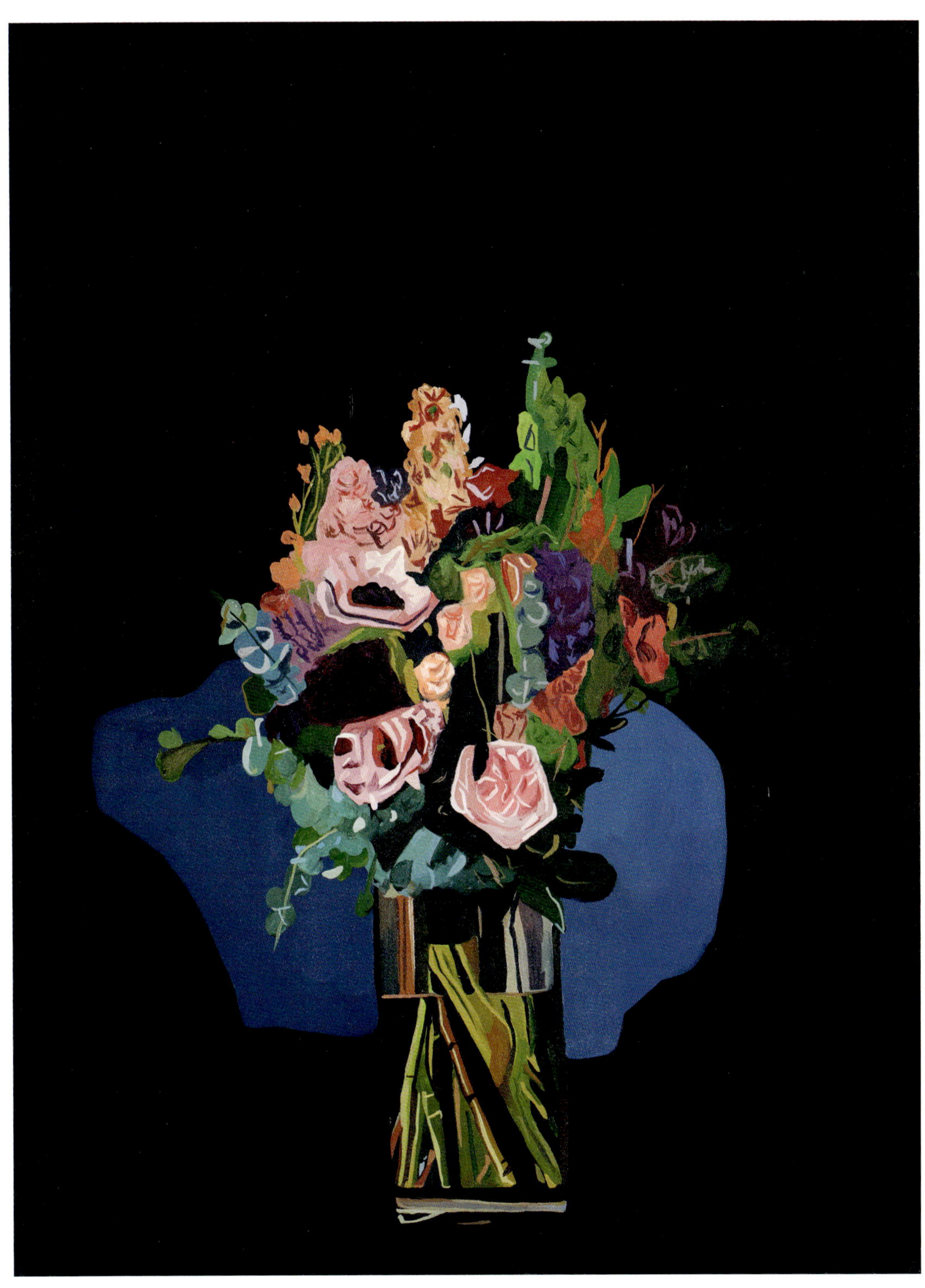

Doron Langberg

Born 1985

Three blousy, showy pink hibiscus flowers take centre-stage in Doron Langberg's painting. Positioned one on top of the other, they tumble down the canvas. The flowers are nestled within a mass of plump leaves and spindly stems, rendered in a palette of greens: forest green, emerald green, juniper green, apple green. While the top of the painting is dark and dense with colour, much of the lower section is left unpainted, giving the painting a spontaneous, provisional quality.

Langberg is best known for their figurative works which centre on queer sexuality and desire. Painted in vibrant tones, they depict male bodies engaged in intimate sexual acts. They connect these intense erotic scenes to their paintings of more mundane, everyday subject matter, saying: 'For me, painting something like flowers, family members, friends hanging out, in addition to extremely explicit queer sexual imagery, humanises the more sexual parts of my work.' In the same way that Langberg's paintings of human figures have a sensual directness, their flowers are depicted up close, as though near enough to smell and touch.

Of equal importance to their subject matter is Langberg's process of making and experience of materials. The artist creates many of their floral works from observation, placing their easel within verdant natural settings. The resulting paint marks – by turns bold, washy, delicate and scribbly – only just suggest the objects they describe. Langberg plays with the limits of our perception: the moment at which an abstract image takes recognisable form. When do smudges of pink paint become a hibiscus flower? When do scratches of green colour become a leaf? ***NP***

Hibiscus 1, 2022
Oil on linen
61 x 45.7 cm
Private collection, London

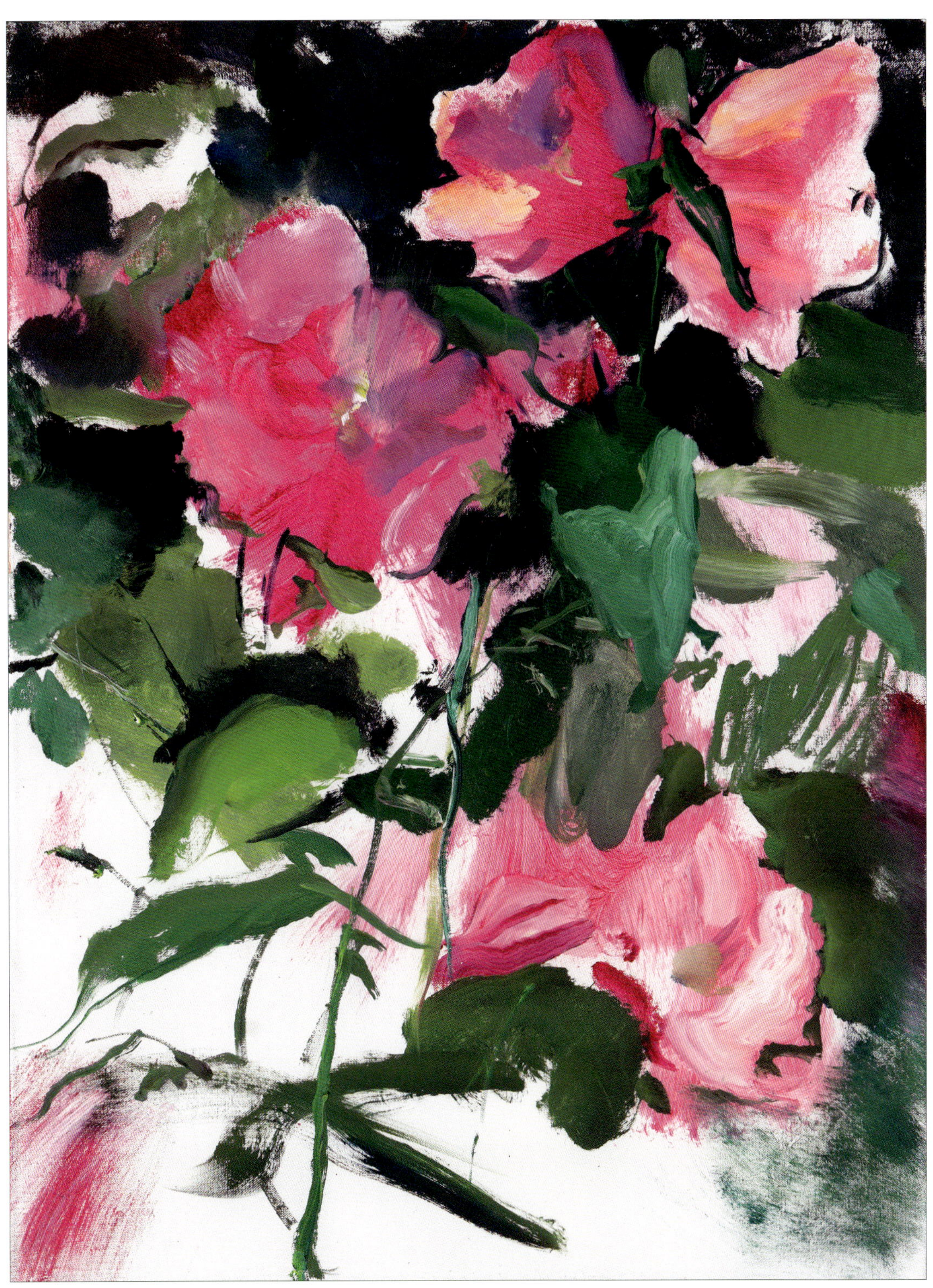

Aubrey Levinthal

Born 1986

A large lilac tulip protrudes from a small green vase, its arching stem extending across the nightstand as though it might topple over. There is a sense of imbalance between the delicate wilting flower and the dark, solid vase that holds it: one is fleeting while the other is permanent. In *Tulip Nightstand (Night)*, Aubrey Levinthal frames the nightstand as a constant stage for the transitory objects that populate our lives.

Levinthal has removed layers of muted green paint using a utility blade to reveal a warm luminescent yellow underneath, creating the impression of light entering the room from the street outside. The view of the flowers and the surrounding objects is obscure, emphasised by the spectral presence of the water glass in front of the vase and tulip head. The artist has placed the large tulip at the centre of the work, its sleepy posture alluding to the human experience of nighttime. It is one of a pair of nightstand paintings by the artist, featuring the same objects in different contexts. Levinthal has said: 'I hope that the paintings register a familiar understanding for viewers. They don't know these nightstands, but they know their own. And that's the goal, to communicate and to commune in that human experience.'

Levinthal's depiction of dappled light and flattened forms is informed by the work of the twentieth-century artists Winifred Nicholson and Gwen John, as well as early Renaissance painters such as Giotto and Masaccio. The objects on the nightstand are engaged with one another in their own realm, separated from the viewer by the edge of the table. Looking on, the viewer is given a window into the intimate space belonging to the room's unknown occupant. *MB*

Tulip Nightstand (Night), 2023
Oil on panel
45.7 x 45.7 cm
Courtesy the artist and
Ingleby Gallery

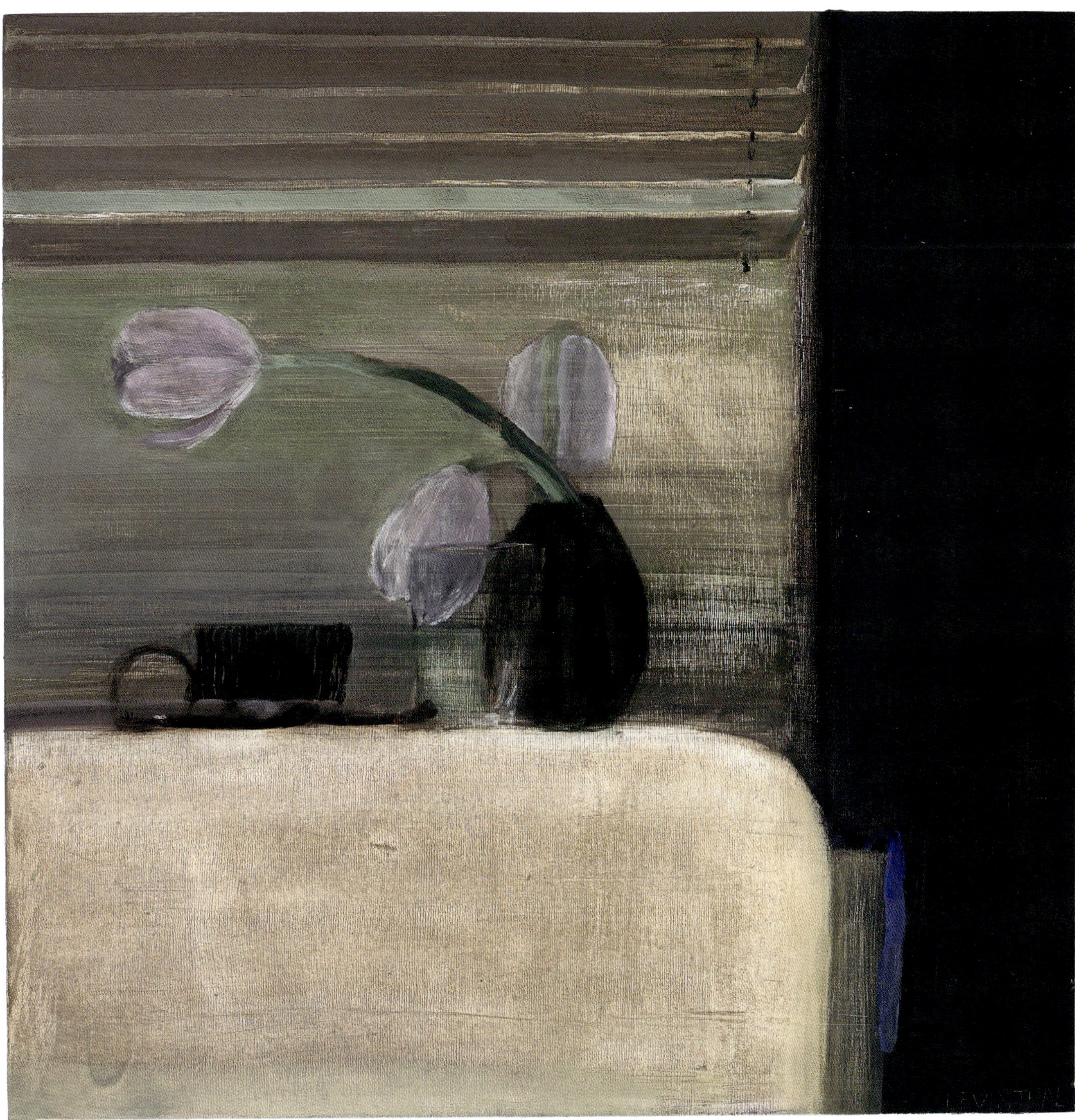

Charles Rennie Mackintosh
1868–1928

Ghostly stems weave between the four fritillaries in Charles Rennie Mackintosh's delicate watercolour painting. The artist captures the characteristic dangling bell shape and purple-and-cream checkerboard pattern of the flowers. The shortest bloom is painted in a surprising pose, however: pointing upwards with its petals spread out. Mackintosh had a firm scientific understanding of plant forms and the ability to depict them with botanical precision. Just as important for him as this, though, was his desire to bring out the beauty of their design and decoration.

Fritillaria was created in an unusually fertile period of artistic making for Mackintosh. It followed two years during which he struggled in his work as an architect and became increasingly dependent on alcohol. In the summer of 1914, he went on holiday to the picturesque town of Walberswick on the Suffolk coast with his wife, the artist Margaret Macdonald. When the First World War broke out a couple of weeks later, they decided to extend their visit and eventually stayed for a full year. During this time he created over 40 studies of both wild and cultivated flowers, each rendered in soft pencil lines and lush washes of watercolour.

'Fritillaria Walberswick 1915 CRM MMM' reads a small, inscribed box at the bottom of the painting. Inspired by their use in Japanese prints, Mackintosh added this 'cartouche box' as a way of situating the painting within a particular time, place and milieu (the initials refer to the artist and his wife). Nestled between two of the fritillaries' tapering stems, it is seamlessly integrated into the painting's composition. In contrast with the regularity of the lettering, however, the plants appear loose and free. Swaying in different directions, the tangled flowers, stems and leaves almost seem like they are moving in an improvised dance. ***NP***

Fritillaria, 1915
Watercolour and pencil on paper
25.3 x 20.2 cm
The Hunterian, University of Glasgow

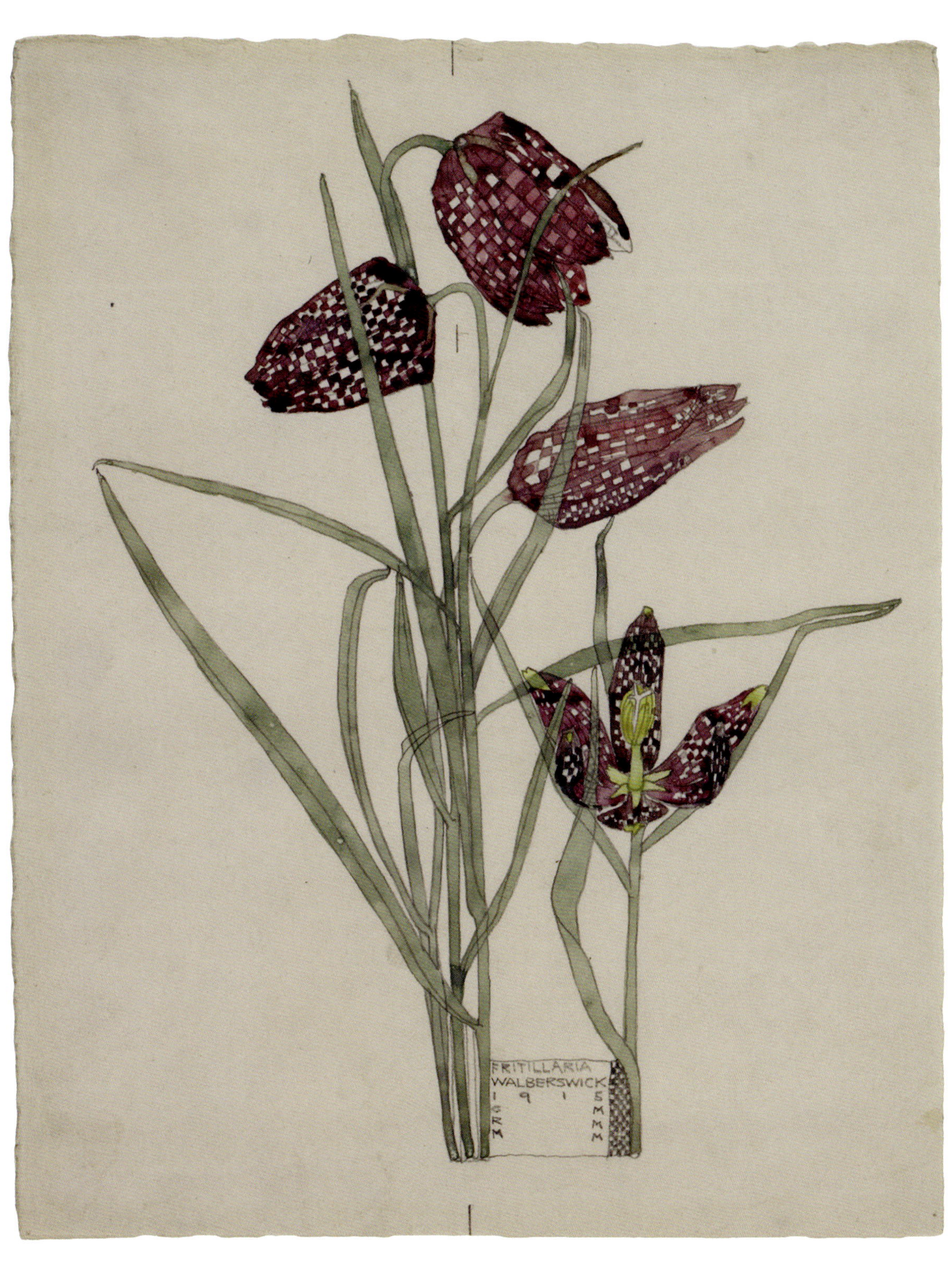
FRITILLARIA
WALBERSWICK
1 9 1 5
CRM
MMM

Rory McEwen
1932–1982

An immaculate tulip is the sole subject of Rory McEwen's watercolour painting. Each of its glossy petals is depicted in meticulous detail. By contrast, the stem has a slightly blurred edge giving it a shimmering, dreamlike quality. McEwen had a lifelong obsession with painting flowers. His childhood sketchbooks are filled with studies of plants and flowers, including a watercolour of a stem of heather created when he was just eight years old. He continued to paint flowers up until his death at the age of 50 in spite of increasing physical pain.

Early in his artistic career McEwen adopted the medium of vellum, a translucent surface traditionally made from calfskin. He would paint plants from life, sometimes employing a scalpel and penknife to make alterations and wearing surgeon's spectacles for fine details. His use of vellum was partly inspired by the work of historic botanical painters, such as Pierre-Joseph Redouté (1759-1840), on whom he wrote his undergraduate dissertation at Cambridge University. McEwen has often been described as a botanical painter himself. Despite their scientific accuracy, however, McEwen's works explore themes outside of this genre, such as decay, disease and the passing of time. Alongside his depictions of perfect specimens, he painted rotting onions, shrivelled peppers and leaves that are barely more than a sprinkling of leaf dust.

This painting is part of a series of 16 illustrations that McEwen created for the book *Tulips & Tulipomania* by Wilfrid Blunt (1977). When he painted this work, McEwen had begun to use more direct, artificial lighting, which gives the flower a surreal luminance, as if it were being spotlit on stage. The painting is a study of colour, structure, texture and touch – a love letter to the natural world. ***NP***

Tulip (Helen Josephine), 1975
Watercolour on vellum
74 x 65.5 cm
Estate of Rory McEwen

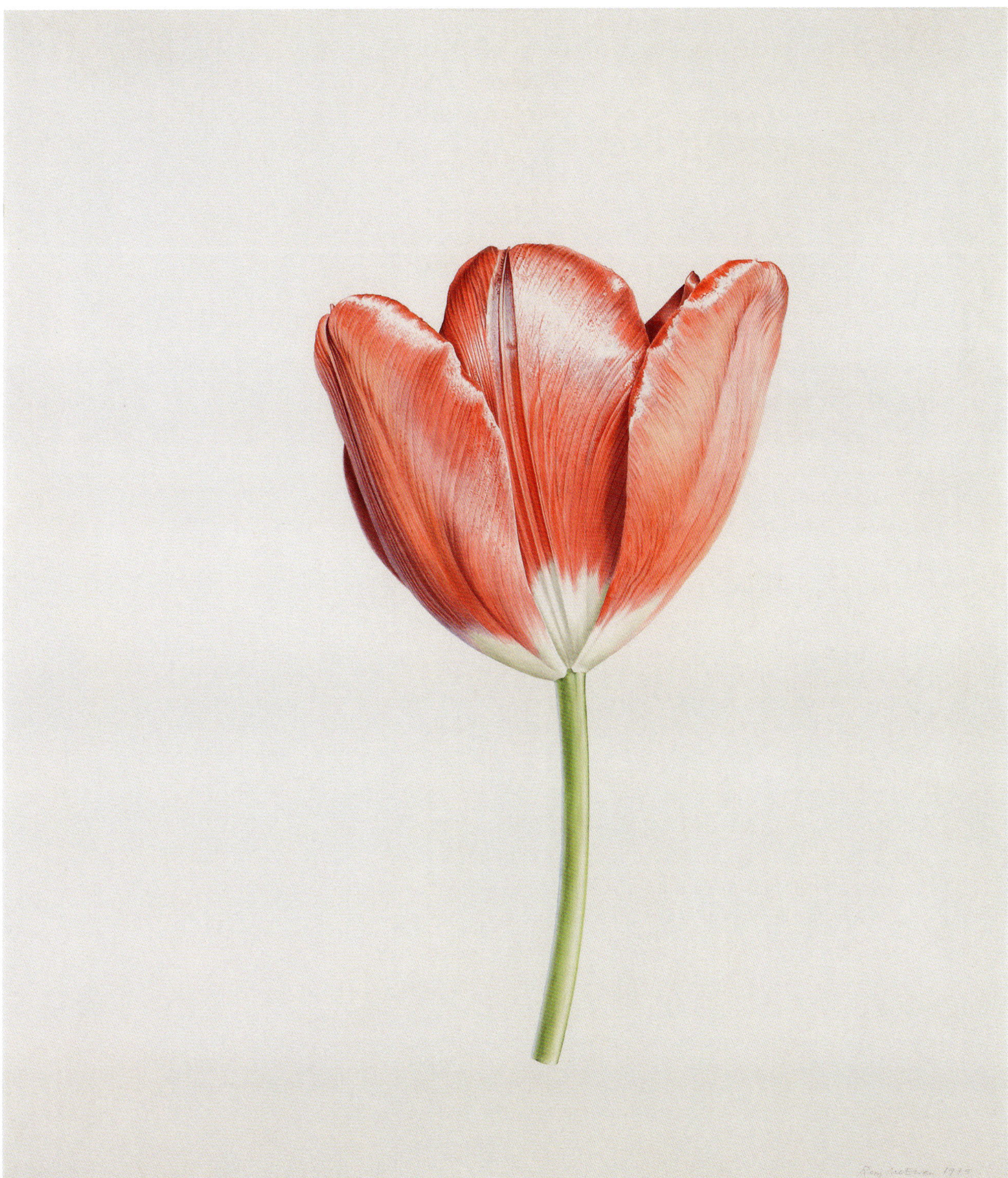

Cedric Morris
1889–1982

Despite their cut state, the irises and tulips of Cedric Morris's arrangement are full of life. Morris's flower paintings have a vitality that challenges the idea of stillness and death inherent to the genre of still life. They are a celebration of beauty in the natural world. The artist collected and bred plants and flowers, painting them with the sensitivity and knowledge with which one might create the portrait of a loved one.

Morris painted this work at the Pound, a Tudor farmhouse in Suffolk where he lived from 1929 to 1940 with his lifelong partner Arthur Lett-Haines. The Pound was where Morris was able to cultivate his work and identity as both an artist and gardener, with each occupation having a profound influence on the other. Throughout the 1930s, Morris increasingly withdrew from the cosmopolitan contemporary art scene, despite the popularity and success of his landscape paintings on the London market. His flower paintings, though not as commercially lucrative, formed a large and important part of his artistic oeuvre.

The Pound became a retreat where fellow artists, writers and bohemians could congregate away from London, revelling in the beauty of the natural surroundings. The gardens tended by Morris were a particular draw for likeminded individuals escaping city life. Whilst at the Pound, Morris began to breed exotic varieties of irises: he grew approximately 1,000 seedlings each year and registered over 90 new varieties. Plants grown in the gardens at the Pound featured more and more in his paintings. Creating these works was an opportunity for the 'artist-plantsman' to become closer acquainted with the plants and flowers that were his fascination. Lovingly documenting each petal and leaf was a way for him to comprehend and commemorate the natural world that he favoured and with which he felt at one. *MB*

Irises and Tulips, 1935
Oil on canvas
61 x 50.8 cm
Private collection, care of
Philip Mould & Company

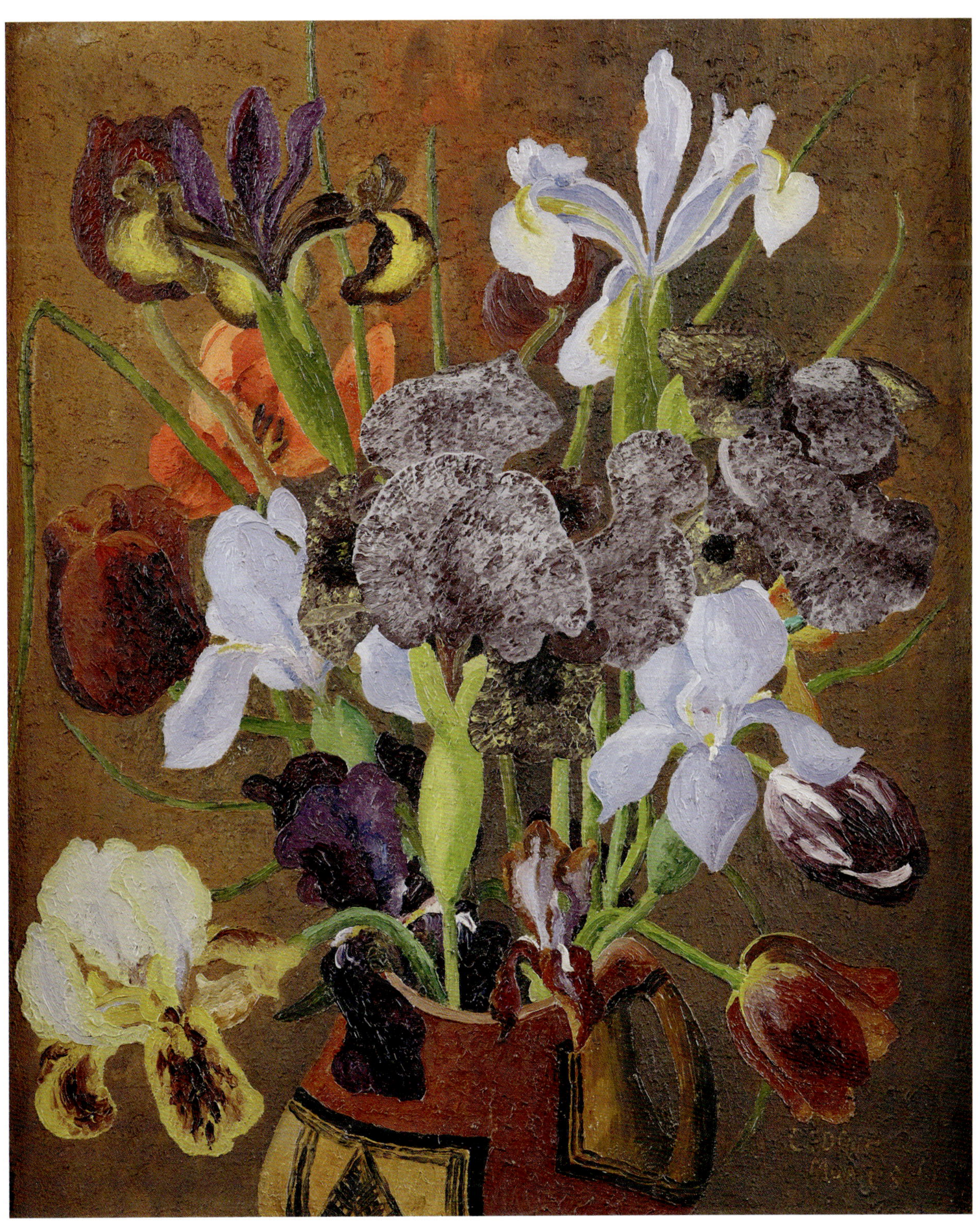

Cassi Namoda

Born 1988

In Cassi Namoda's vivid painting, the pale blue petals of a single flower completely fill the canvas and imaginatively extend beyond its edges. The flower's centre, an earthen red from which delicate lines radiate outwards, is surrounded by inner petals painted in creamy white with touches of pink. A background of the same red visually connects the centre with the periphery.

The painting is one of several that celebrate the birth of Namoda's young daughter, Arafah: 'I made my first flower painting in the spring my daughter was born. That year the rains were long and drenching, and then she arrived almost ceremonially, in the first full sunlight of the season's turning. I was deeply moved by the timing of her birth, how it mirrored the blossoming outside. It felt as though she had come with the flowers.'

Now living in Italy, Namoda was born in Mozambique, which remains a living presence for the artist: a place of memories, emotions, ideas, images and imagination, which all infuse her work. Her flower was inspired by a common variety that the artist recalls seeing as a child on her grandmother's land. The vertical form of the canvas is suggestive of a portrait, while the subject, as if magnified, highlights the richly tactile surface of the painting, which was created over many days through the gradual application of layers of oil pigment.

For the artist, the image of the flower is a space for contemplation and may hold many meanings. The composition and process of making the painting reflect 'the quiet formative moments that shape maternal identity, its rhythms and attentiveness'. The flower is not a detached, ornamental object in Namoda's painting, but rather an expression of human experience. Namoda seeks to capture the feeling of a new world of motherhood and of the deepest love. ***AN***

Arafah Gaza's Arrival, 2025
Oil on canvas
48.3 x 30.5 cm
Courtesy the artist and
Xavier Hufkens, Brussels

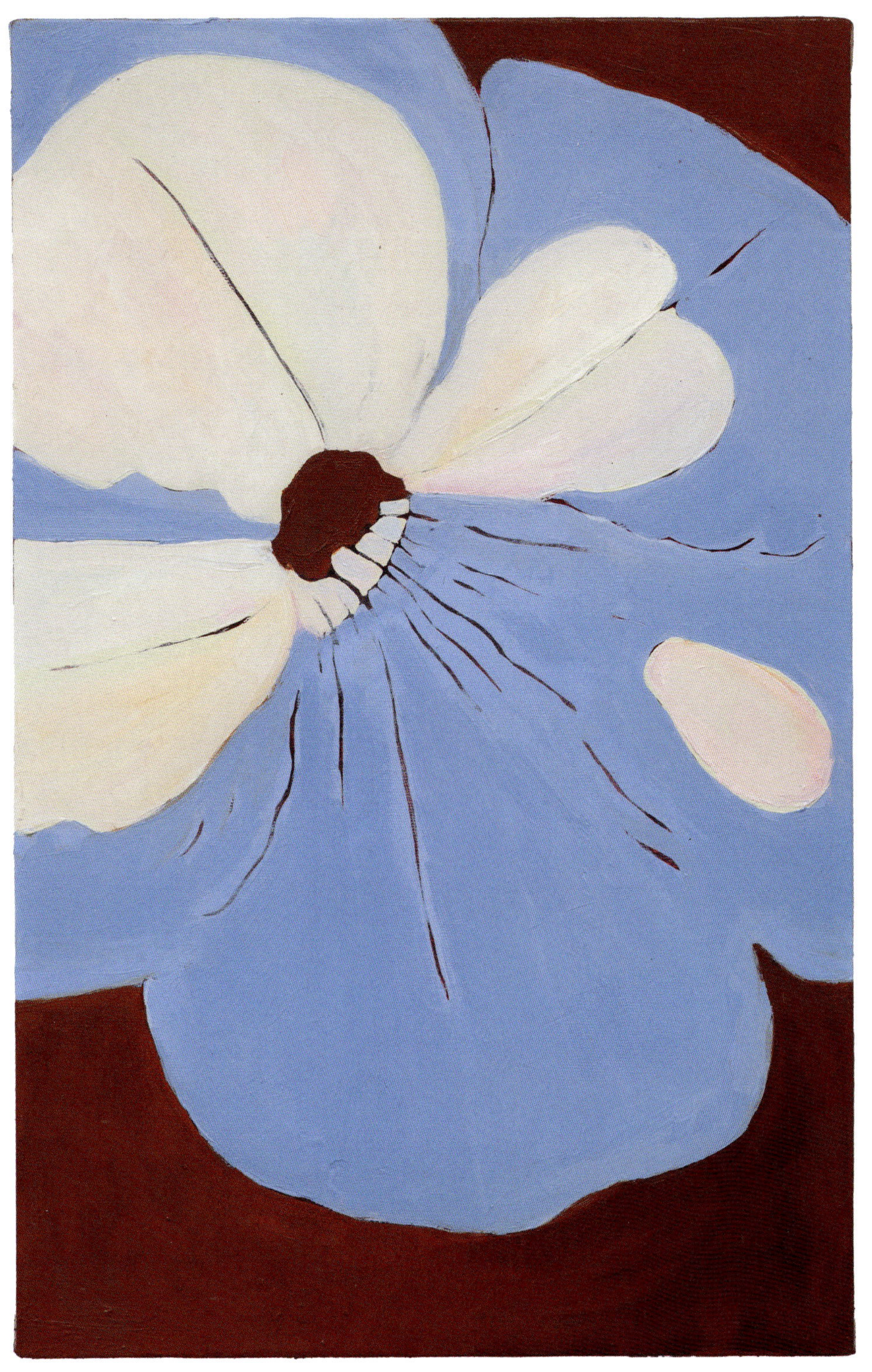

Mary Newcomb

1922–2008

Three vases, each containing six violas, are the subject of Mary Newcomb's lively painting. The vases hold flowers of different colours – lilac, black and white – but the violas themselves are depicted uniformly, with each of their five open petals painted with a single brushstroke. The fullness and vitality of the flowers contrasts with the sketchy, ghostly vessels that contain them. Whereas one might expect the vases to have a certain solidity in comparison with the fragile flowers, in Newcomb's painting this relationship is reversed: the permanent objects are represented as ethereal and ephemeral, while the flowers are robust in form and colour.

Studies of flowers formed an important aspect of Newcomb's work, which centred on representations of rural life. After studying and teaching science in her early adulthood, she turned to painting when she moved to East Anglia in 1950. Living in seclusion in the countryside, she was able to be closely attuned to her natural locale. Working outdoors, Newcomb captured both the minute and monumental aspects of country life in her drawings and handwritten notes. She would then distil her observations and reimagine them in paint within the confines of her studio.

Six Violas is emblematic of Newcomb's direct, but subtle style. The flowers are the focus of the work, while their containers fade into the ambiguous background. The realm that these violas inhabit is oblique, but the thin rectangles that frame the vases suggest the architectural structure of a home and the cut state of the flowers implies a human presence. The rich green background, however, recalls the natural environment from which they came. This adds a sense of spontaneity; the violas have just been picked and are being transferred to their new location. The painting encompasses the flowers' fleeting and temporary state of being. ***MB***

Six Violas, 1985
Oil on canvas
48.2 cm x 58.5 cm
Private collection, care of
Crane Kalman Gallery

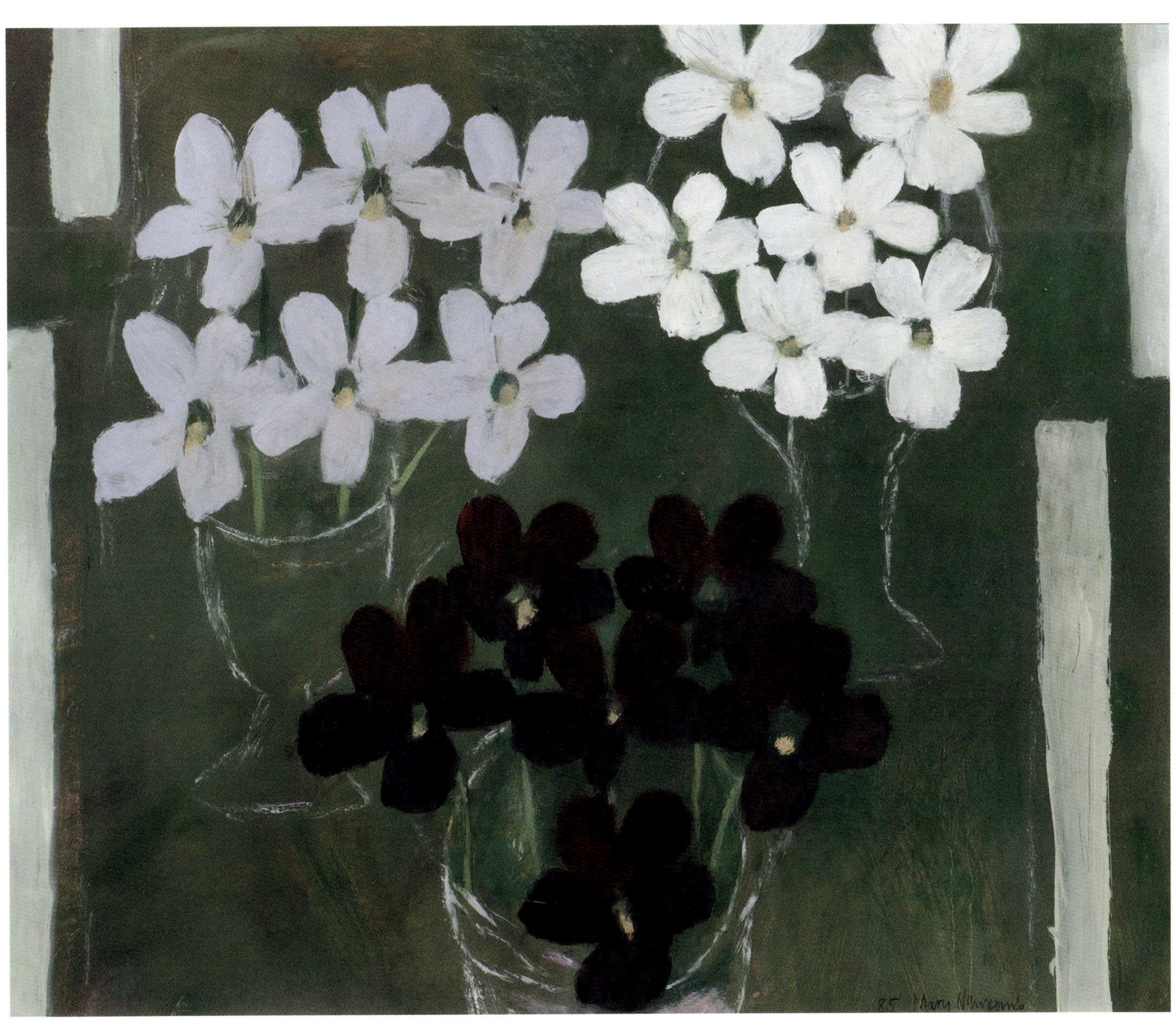

William Nicholson

1872–1949

An elegant bloom of pink peonies in a crisp, clear glass vase occupies the centre of William Nicholson's understated composition. Light seems to radiate from the flowers themselves as they cast a dramatic, dark shadow behind them. Nicholson's still-life paintings often depicted flowers from his own garden or bouquets given by his friends. Painted at the same time as a large commission in Paris, where the artist created complex historical and imagined scenes across 50 glass panels, *Pink Peonies* shows the artist's delight in the simplicity of his subject.

Nicholson's flower paintings are characterised by a stillness and tranquillity. The viewer is drawn into a world removed from peripheral distractions. Up until the turn of the twentieth century, Nicholson had been a pioneering graphic illustrator, producing striking posters and witty woodcut prints. Once he turned to painting, his style was largely indebted to that of the 'Old Masters', such as Rembrandt and Velázquez, particularly their attention to detail and the atmospheric effects of *chiaroscuro* – the use of strong contrasts between light and shade to create a sense of volume, three-dimensionality and emotional intensity.

In this painting, Nicholson creates a sense of harmony between light and shade. The dark shadow cast by the light-pink peonies brings a dramatic quality to an otherwise simple scene. The presence of the peonies within the painting dominates the domestic surroundings, which are only hinted at through the wooden tabletop on which they are placed. The shallow perspective and absence of any other objects enabled Nicholson to create a study of his subject with a warmth and sensitivity that radiates from within the flowers. *MB*

Pink Peonies, 1913
Oil on canvas
40.6 x 33 cm
Private collection

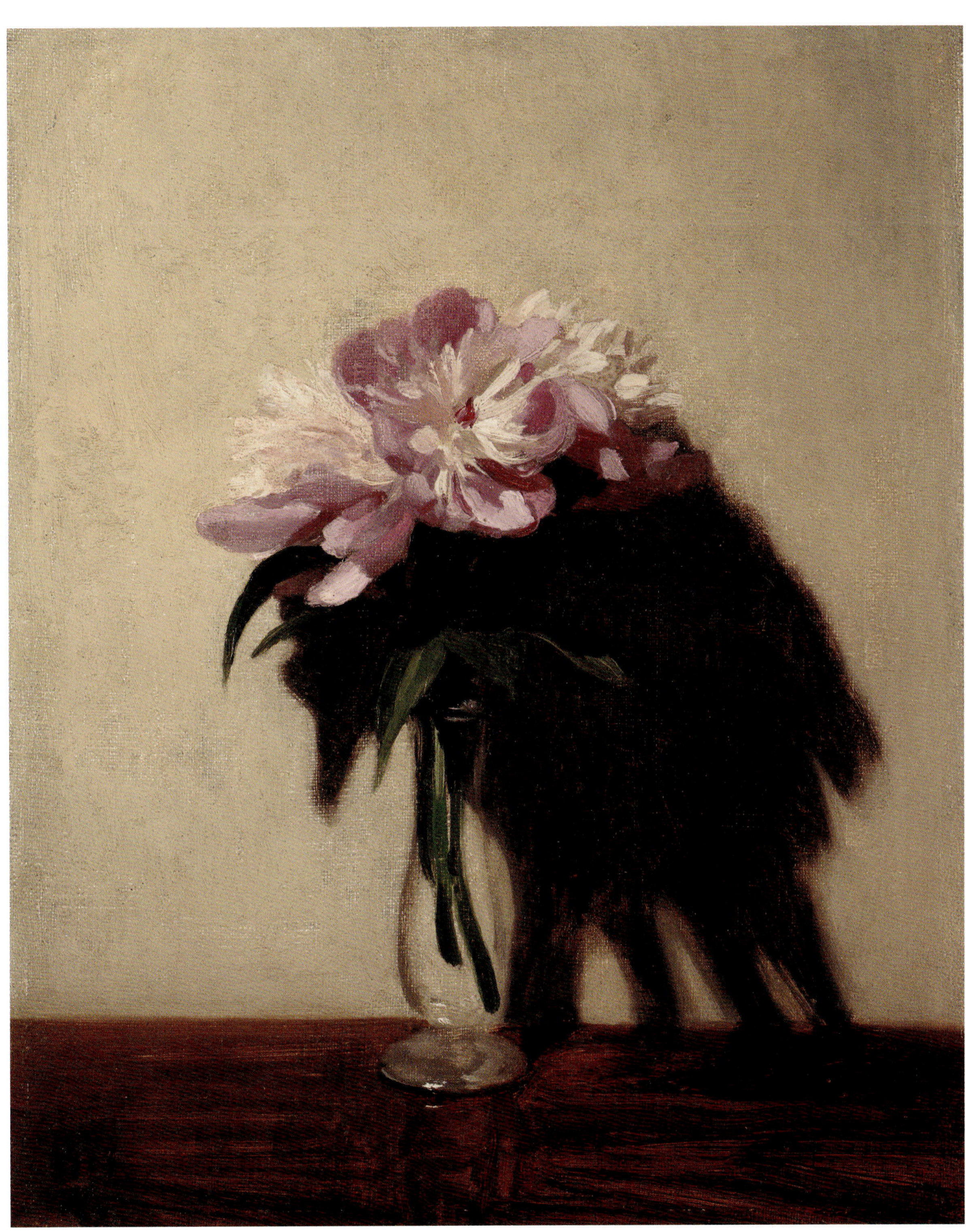

Winifred Nicholson

1893–1981

A sturdy jug holds a sparse, delicate array of flowers in Winifred Nicholson's *White Campion*. In the centre is the tallest white campion, which tapers up past the horizon line into the sky, its five petals splayed and milky-white. It is surrounded by smaller white campions and on the right side by ribwort plantains, recognisable for their distinctive spiky flower heads and whirl of white stamens. In Nicholson's composition these common wildflowers, often found in grasslands and on roadsides, are given the same importance as a cultivated ornamental bouquet.

Flowers were the subject to which Nicholson returned most frequently over the course of her 60-year artistic career. In her 1969 essay *The Flower's Response*, she wrote: 'my paint brush always gives a tremor of pleasure when I let it paint a flower'. Often she depicted the flowers in pots, bowls and vases set on a windowsill overlooking a landscape, creating a conversation between the domestic interior space and the world beyond.

White Campion was painted in the coastal village of St Bees in Cumberland (now Cumbria), where for a short time during the Second World War Nicholson's son Jake attended the local school. The island silhouetted in the background of the painting is the Isle of Man, seen across the Irish Sea. There is a subtle blurring between the jug of flowers in the painting's foreground and the seascape behind. The decorative features on the jug, with their maritime subjects, are painted in the same luminous blue colour as the sea. One of the stems in the bouquet of wildflowers has curlicued ends, connecting it with shapes of the energetic sea waves. Nicholson transforms the real-life view into a vision of colour and light, imbued with memory and emotion. *NP*

White Campion, circa 1940s
Oil on canvas
61 x 61 cm
Private collection, courtesy
Crane Kalman Gallery

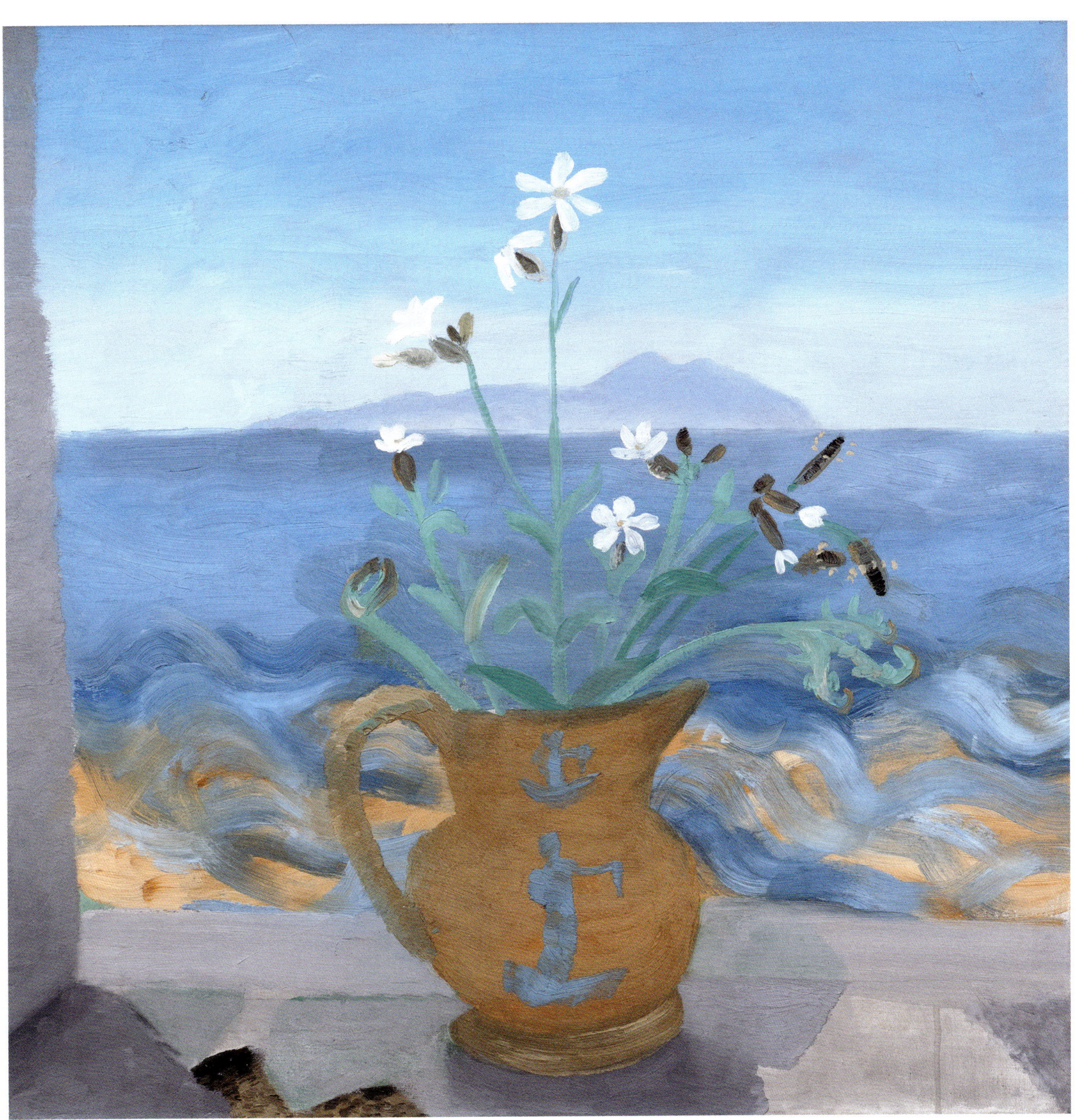

Chris Ofili

Born 1968

A rainbow-coloured plant takes up almost the entire composition of Chris Ofili's *Untitled (Afromuse)*. Stems and leaves extend out across the page and a resplendent flower blossoms at the top. On either side of it are the heads of a man and a woman, emerging from the plant as though they themselves are flowers. Elements of their faces reflect the colouring of the plant: the woman's lipstick and eye shadow echo the pinks and greens of the flower, while the man's beard merges with the black leaves. In contrast with the vibrant painted imagery, a faint pencil under-drawing marks out an amorphous shape beneath.

This painting is part of a series of watercolours Ofili made between 1995 and 2005 that depict imaginary people, flowers and birds, inspired by a range of references including art history, pop culture and the artist's personal memories. The figures have elaborate hairstyles and extravagant clothing, while the flowers are made up of luminous colours and fantastical shapes. Ofili has described these works as being rooted in the process of their making: 'it's about a formal exercise – the enjoyment of the type of paper, the consistency of the watercolour, the softness of the brush, the way the paint will soak into or flow across the paper.'

In this work there is the sense that the paint has its own agency. The colours merge directly into one another, forming surprising composite tones and watery plumes of paint. The composition brings together the real and fanciful in a similarly fluid way. With its human appendages, the flower is cast in the role of universal life-giver – a joyful, all-encompassing growth, born out of watercolour paint. ***NP***

Untitled (Afromuse), 2005
Watercolour and
graphite on paper
32.2 x 21 cm
Courtesy the artist and
Victoria Miro

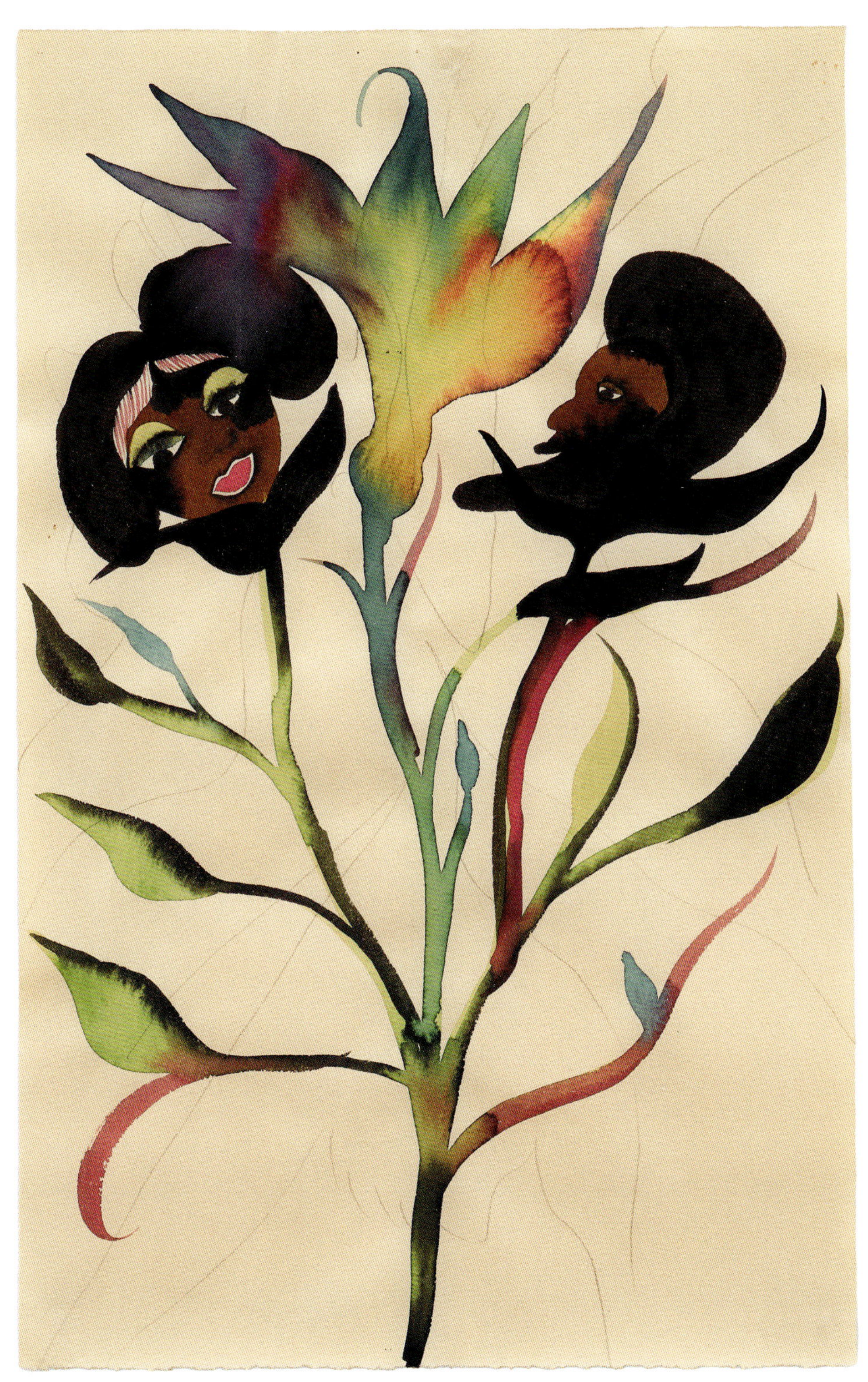

Jennifer Packer

Born 1984

Jennifer Packer's painting of a bunch of chrysanthemums has a feverish, fiery quality. Packer experiments with the capabilities of paint. Her rapid brushstrokes create the impression of dense crimson petals and tapering green-brown stems. Some lines are applied with wet, viscous paint, while others are faint and dry. In places, she has intervened with her own hand, leaving the trace of visible finger marks.

Packer began painting flowers in 2012, the year she graduated from art school. Her first flower painting, depicting a bouquet that she had been given by a friend, marked a departure from her usual practice of painting Black figures. She has said: 'What I found was that I didn't feel the need to make those paintings carry the weight of the question of what Blackness is.' As the Black Lives Matter movement brought to light the killings of innocent Black men and women by the US police, Packer's floral paintings took on a more urgent political meaning. She began to dedicate them to the victims of police brutality, seeing them as symbols of loss and mourning, like funerary bouquets.

Unlike many flower paintings that are situated within a domestic context, Packer's chrysanthemums are set against a simple yellow background. The flowers extend upwards and outwards, filling the whole composition. With their expansiveness, they limit information about their surroundings. There is a sense of withholding. Rather than representing a specific bunch of flowers, Packer creates an emotional presence, an act of memorialisation. ***NP***

Chrysanthemums, 2015
Oil on canvas
45.5 x 37.5 cm
The Fitzwilliam Museum,
University of Cambridge,
bought with the support of
Kemal Has and
Tala Cingillioglu, 2024

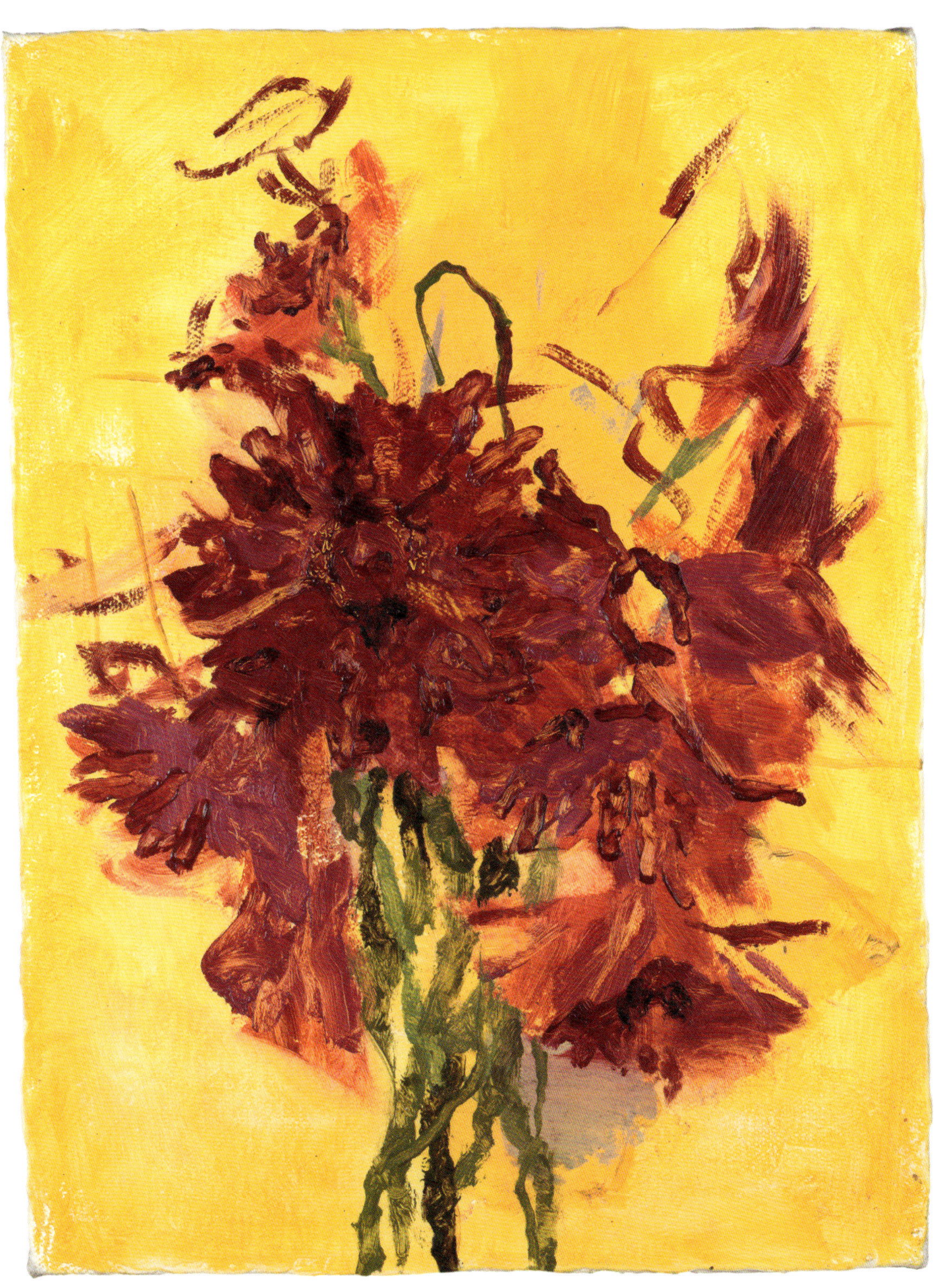

Celia Paul

Born 1959

A branch of tall, commanding delphiniums glides across the paper in Celia Paul's *Delphinium, February 14th.* The artist's delicate use of watery pigments and the dewy appearance of the petals situates the flowers within the wind and rain of winter. The small bursts of yellow create the impression of warm dappled light falling on the flowers, perhaps suggesting the coming of spring. Yet the light also seems to radiate from the flowers themselves, lending the painting a spectral feel.

Paul pins sheets of paper to an easel or drawing board as she paints her compositions. This vertical orientation transfers the agency from the artist to her medium, allowing the ink and watercolour to drip, smudge and move across the surface without the artist's interference. Paul creates her works on paper in response to special moments and events that she wants to commemorate. As a sequence, they accumulate into a form of diary. Works with dates that carry strong, personal meaning for Paul are not always made explicit to the viewer. However this painting is inscribed towards the lower right corner with its title – *Delphinium, February 14th* – dating it to St Valentine's Day.

Paul's paintings often depict personal subjects, such as emotionally or psychologically charged portraits of family members, as well as exploring feelings of love, loss and grief. The large scale of *Delphinium, February 14th* magnifies the flowers in a way that feels deeply intimate. Paul has commented that 'flowers very often mark occasions: births, weddings, funerals, public holidays, saints' days'. Her depiction of delphiniums demonstrates the way in which paintings of flowers, as well as the flowers themselves, can represent complex human emotions on occasions that are both shared by all and profoundly individual. ***MB***

Delphinium, February 14th, 2024
Watercolour and
pastel on paper
101.6 x 66 cm
Courtesy the artist
and Victoria Miro

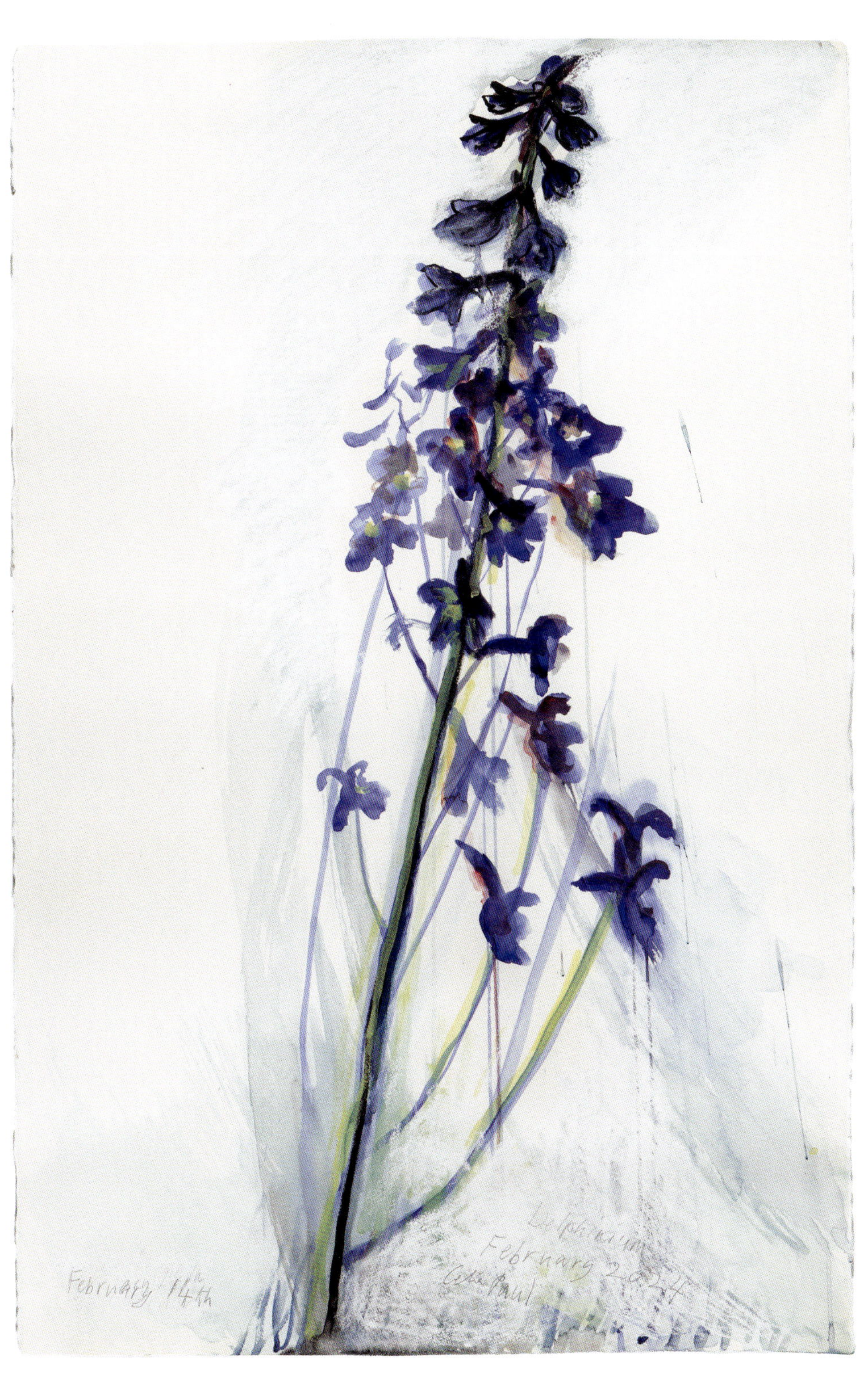
February 14th
Delphinium
February 2024
Paul

Bryan Pearce

1927–2007

A sprightly arrangement of red tulips and yellow daffodils springs and sways in a water jug. The heavy orange outlines of the flowers, window ledge and surrounding landscape give the painting a flattened, geometric quality, reducing the flowers to their simplest colours and forms. Each petal, leaf and stem has its place within the framework of the canvas.

Pearce was encouraged to paint by his mother, who was also an artist, for therapeutic purposes. He was born with Phenylketonuria, a rare condition affecting the development of the brain. In 1953 he began painting watercolours of still-life arrangements composed by his mother, as well as local scenes of St Ives where he lived all his life. He exhibited regularly at the Penwith Gallery and joined the Newlyn Society of Artists in 1959. His approach to painting was slow and methodical, not influenced by the work of others but instead focused on expressing his personal experience of the world.

St Ives had been an important place for Modernist artists of the previous generation, including Alfred Wallis, Christopher Wood, Winifred Nicholson and Barbara Hepworth, with Wood and Nicholson depicting similar still lifes of flowers with an onward view of the Atlantic Ocean. For Pearce, the view of a vase of flowers, set against the Cornish coastline from the window, captures a sense of the artist's contentment and joy in his surroundings; clear, effortless and beautiful. *MB*

Still Life, 1987
Oil on board
61 x 50.8 cm
Jenna Burlingham Gallery

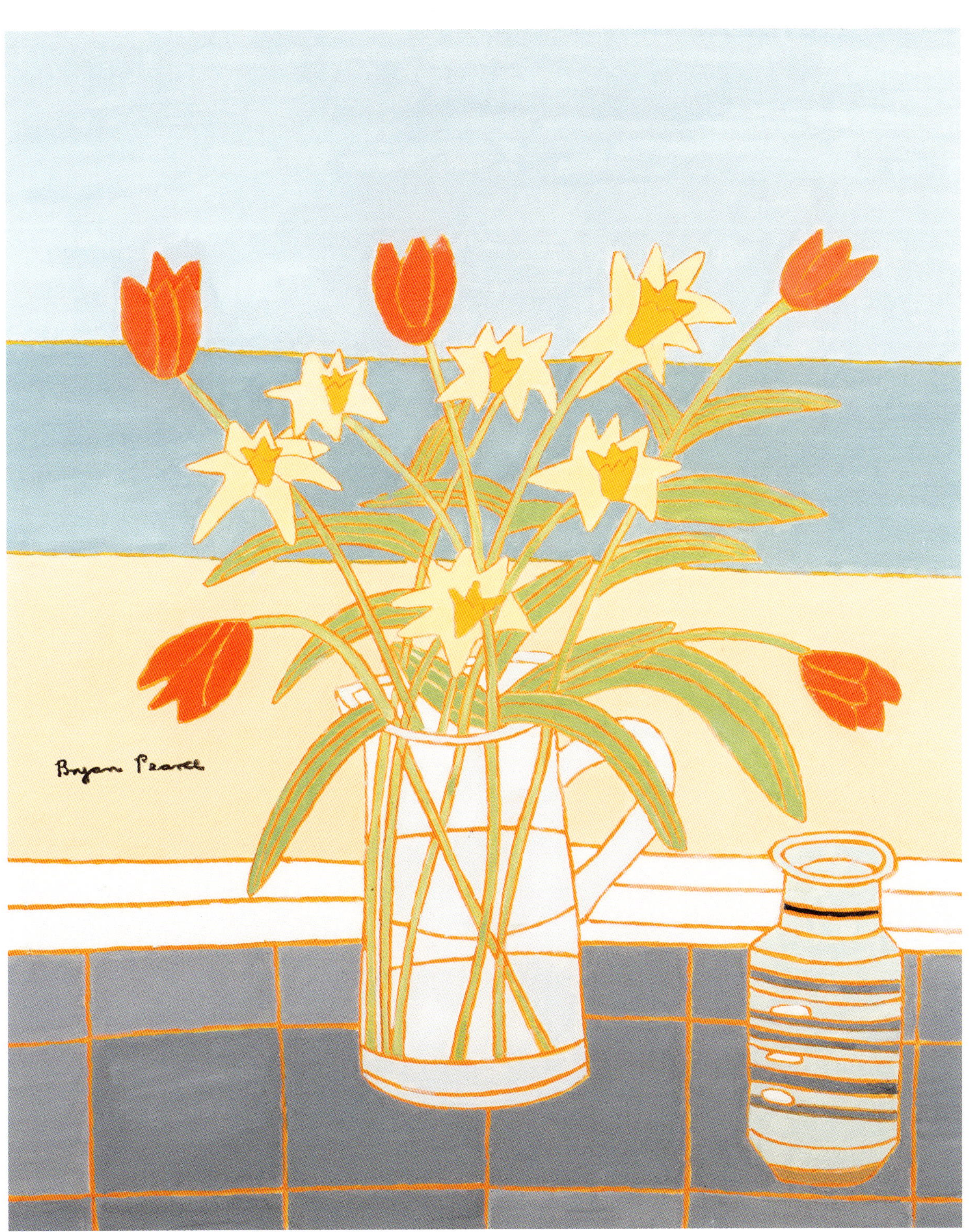
Bryan Pearce

Emma Prempeh

Born 1996

Marigolds emerge out of sweeping, washy brushstrokes and precise, intricate lines in Emma Prempeh's dramatic floral painting. The shape of the marigold florets is brought out by marks of Schlag metal – an imitation gold leaf that subtly changes in appearance as it rusts. The painting is therefore subject to slow, material change in the same way that the flowers it depicts will inevitably wilt and decay.

Prempeh painted *Study of Marigolds (Uganda)* while spending time on her partner Alim Karmali's family farm in Kampala, Uganda. It marked a new direction in her practice, which mostly encompasses large-scale portraits and interior scenes representing her experiences of home, memory and belonging as a child of diaspora. In Uganda she felt a deep reconnection with nature and was inspired to paint leaves, trees and flowers. She has said: 'I remember thinking: this is the beginning; this is where the land starts to grow and flourish.'

In this painting the marigolds, often associated with the sun's warmth, have a primal energy as they burst forth from the dark background. Like in many of Prempeh's works, blackness is used to deliberate effect. Throughout her practice Prempeh experiments with different tones of black to depict shadows and silhouettes and create a mood of nostalgia and longing. Often forming the compositional backdrop, earthy dark-hued colour is applied to the canvas in loose, fluid brush marks, leaving behind visible drips of paint. Prempeh connects her use of these colours with celestial bodies such as stars and black holes. Against the surrounding darkness, the gold-red marigolds stand out like balls of colour and light, as though part of a cosmic landscape. ***NP***

Study of Marigolds (Uganda), 2024
Oil, acrylic and
Schlag metal on canvas
76 x 61 cm
Collection of
Alexander V. Petalas

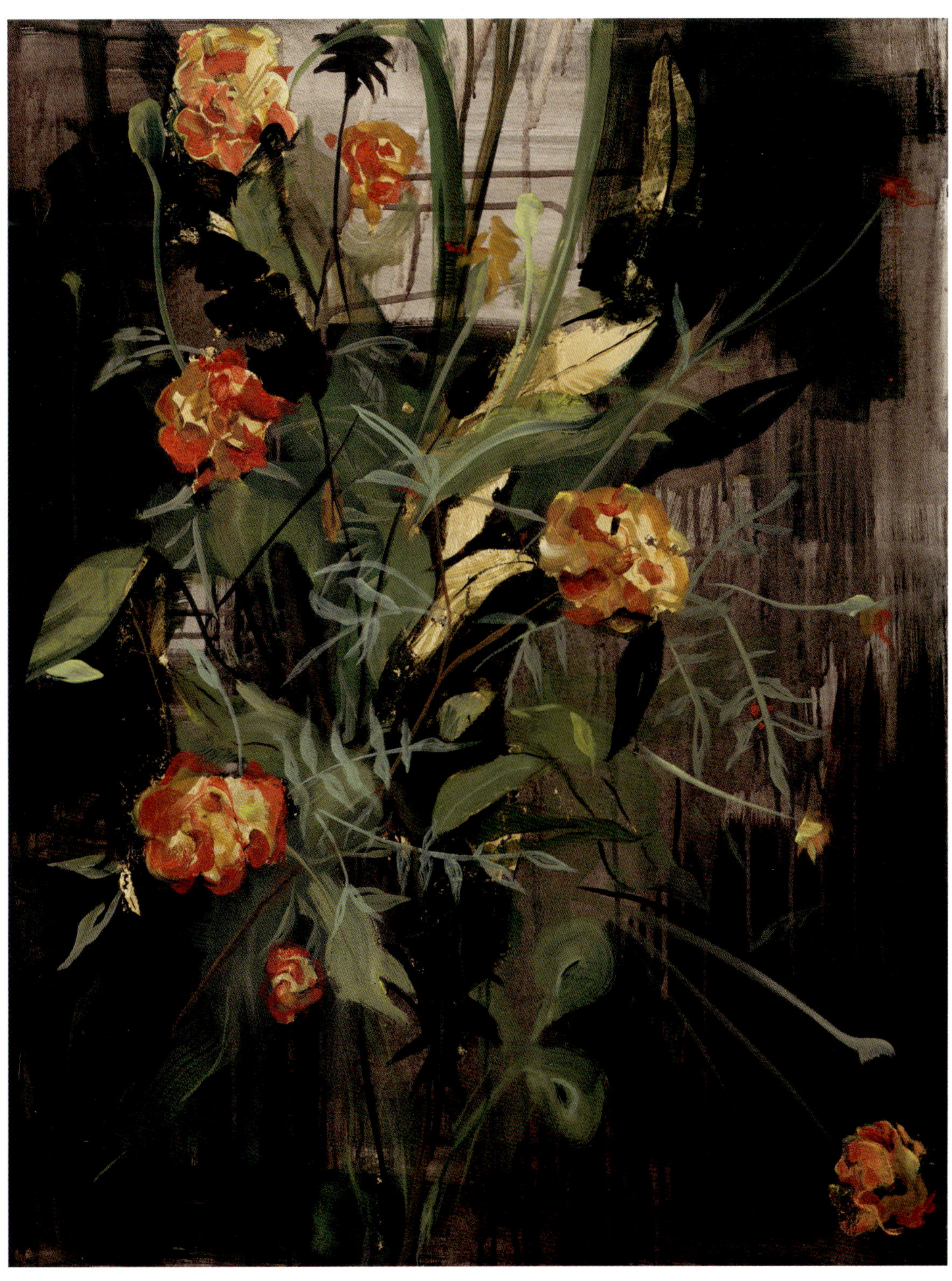

Bianca Raffaella

Born 1992

Emerging through the layers of paint like an apparition, the flowers in *Waxflower* have an ethereal quality. Bianca Raffaella maps out the composition of her works using her fingers, working the paint as if it were sculpture. The flowers in the centre of the canvas slowly reveal themselves to the viewer.

For Raffaella, flower paintings represent the way in which she encounters the world. As a partially sighted artist, she depicts flowers as a response to the physical, tactile qualities of the blooms she has in her studio. The paintings combine her memory of seeing flowers with the intimate feeling of holding one in her hand. The flowers appear both in and out of focus to reflect the constant motion of Raffaella's vision. They capture a fleeting image or moment. By holding small, delicate flowers in her hands, the artist discovers information contained within them and translates it onto the canvas. Flowers reveal themselves to her in a similar way to the raised surfaces of Braille – there is a language of texture in her depictions of them. Building up layers and modelling the perceived shapes of flowers, she conveys her intimate knowledge of her subject.

Flower paintings are a respite for Raffaella: a symbol of comfort and new growth. Her experience of flowers through touch is slow and intimate. In a world dominated by the immediacy of looking, Raffaella's work encourages the viewer to slow down and rest upon the image, to decipher the layers of muted colours and trace the lines created by her hands. *MB*

Waxflower, 2025
Acrylic on board
84 x 59 cm
Courtesy the artist and Flowers Gallery, London/Hong Kong

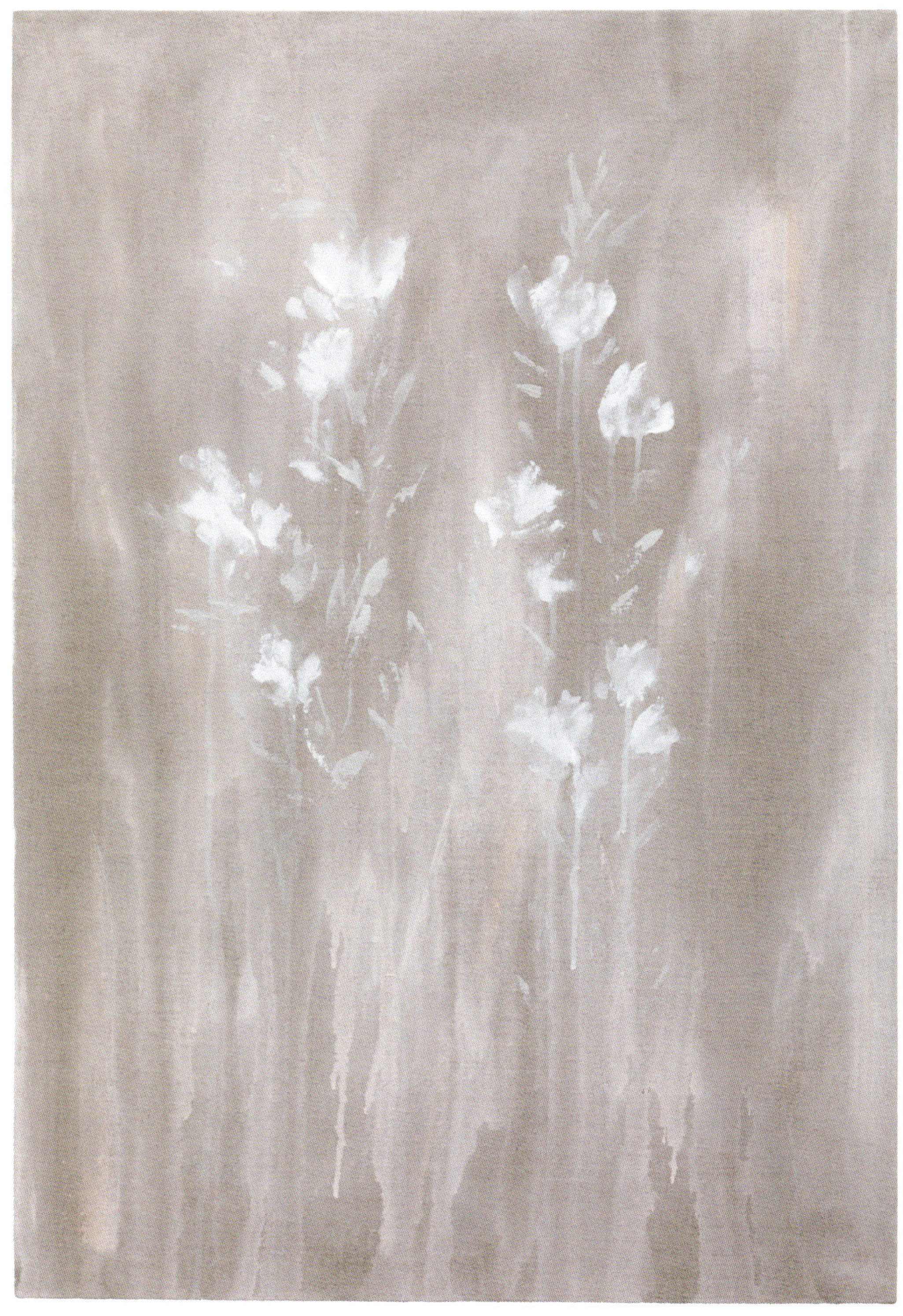

Eric Ravilious

1903–1942

Ironbridge Interior places two different forms of flower painting in conversation with one another, like a double portrait. The flowers on the table in the foreground appear lively, as if they have been freshly picked from the garden that can be glimpsed through the window. Hung on the wall is a painting-within-the painting, depicting perhaps a vase of flowers that preceded the current one. The faint clouds at the top of this painting, as well as the wilted appearance of the flowers, suggest a state of transition between life and death.

Eric Ravilious painted this work at Ironbridge House in Essex, where he lived with his wife Tirzah Garwood from 1940. The house was owned by Labour politician John Strachey and Ravilious would paint interior views of the house and the surrounding landscape and gift them to Strachey as a way of reducing their rent.

When this painting was made, Ravilious was working as a commissioned war artist, painting landscapes filled with barbed wire and machinery, control rooms and airfields. However, there is an element of freedom in his depictions of Ironbridge, as they were not intended to be seen in a public setting and therefore provide an insight into the intimate domesticity of the house. Many paintings of the house contain objects that hint at the fact that the occupant of the room has temporarily left and is about to return. *Ironbridge Interior*, on the other hand, possesses a distinct stillness: the room is sparse and the empty chair appears at odds with the animated bouquet of flowers on the table. The painting of deteriorating flowers on the wall foreshadows the poignancy of Ravilious's death the following year. *MB*

Ironbridge Interior, 1941
Watercolour and pencil on paper
46 x 57.7 cm
On loan from a private collection
via Towner Eastbourne

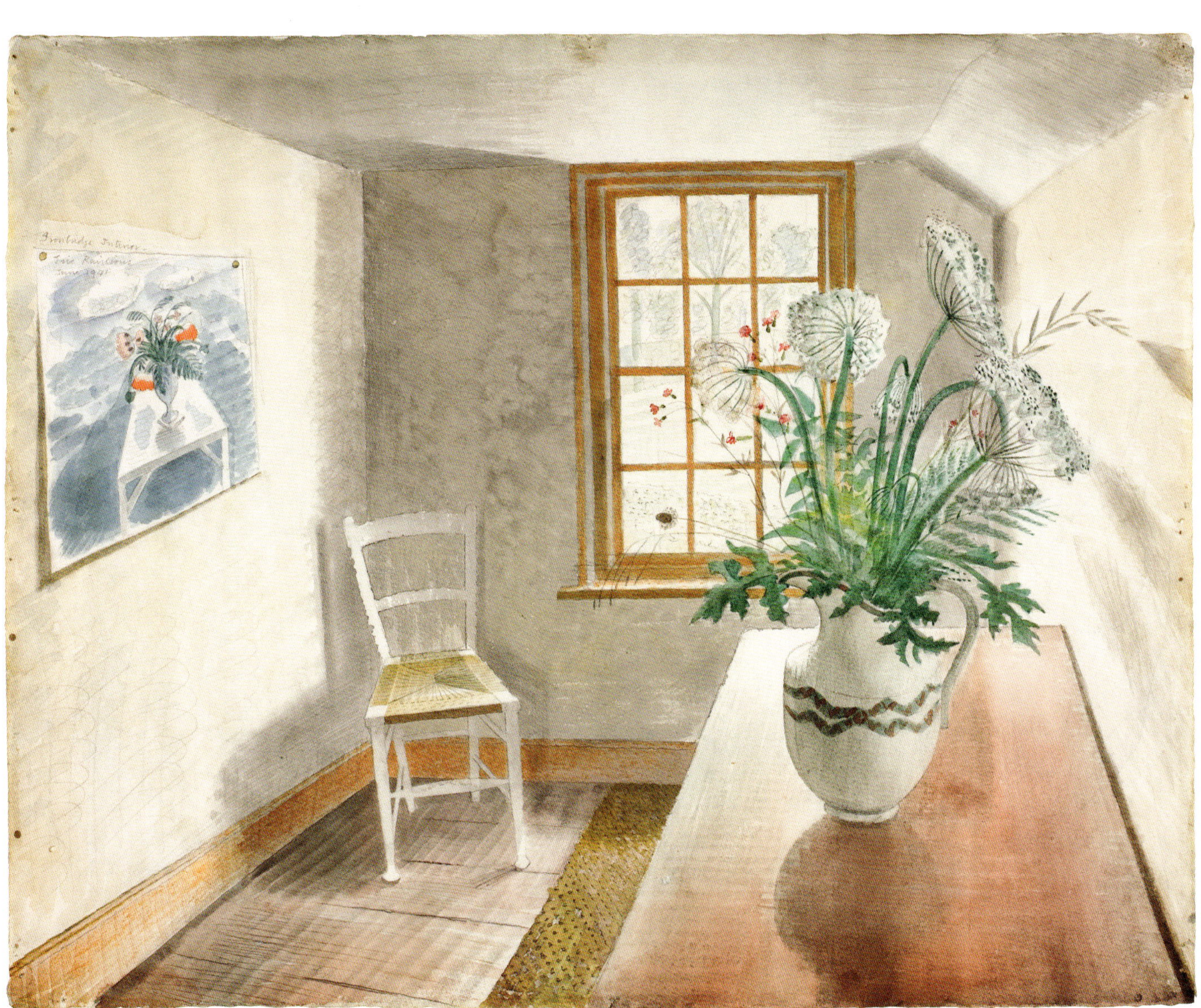

Anne Redpath
1895–1965

Luminous white cyclamen glow amongst the dark shadows in Anne Redpath's painting. The flowers seem to float in space, as if appearing out of thin air. Free from conventional perspective and form, the painting draws minimal distinction between leaf and stem, foreground and background. Only the petals have a defined presence. Though they give the impression of whiteness, the flowers are in fact made up of a wide palette of colours, including lilac, blue and ochre. The composition is created through numerous layers of thick paint, giving it a sense of energy and motion, as well as a sculptural quality.

The genre of still life provided the means for Redpath to experiment with her approach to painting throughout her artistic career. As a student in 1919 she travelled to Florence and Siena, where she became strongly influenced by the layered technique of fresco painting and depictions of the divine in early Italian art. Following her move to Edinburgh in 1949, she would visit exhibitions at the Royal Scottish Academy featuring works by Édouard Vuillard, Paul Gauguin and Amedeo Modigliani, which encouraged her focus on representing interior spaces.

In Redpath's paintings, the depiction of man-made objects evolves into a form of portraiture. The meaning and purpose of the objects are made evident through the interiors they inhabit, from domestic environments to religious settings. Her compositions often include personal belongings that characterise an individual, such as ornaments, clothes and carefully arranged bouquets of flowers. However, in *White Cyclamen*, there is no evidence of an interior. The flowers inhabit a realm of their own, unrelated to other objects, so that their presence becomes all-encompassing. Redpath uses the genre of flower painting to explore and extend the act of painting itself. *MB*

White Cyclamen, 1962
Oil on canvas
63.3 x 76.4 cm
Aberdeen City Council
(Aberdeen Archives, Gallery & Museums collections)

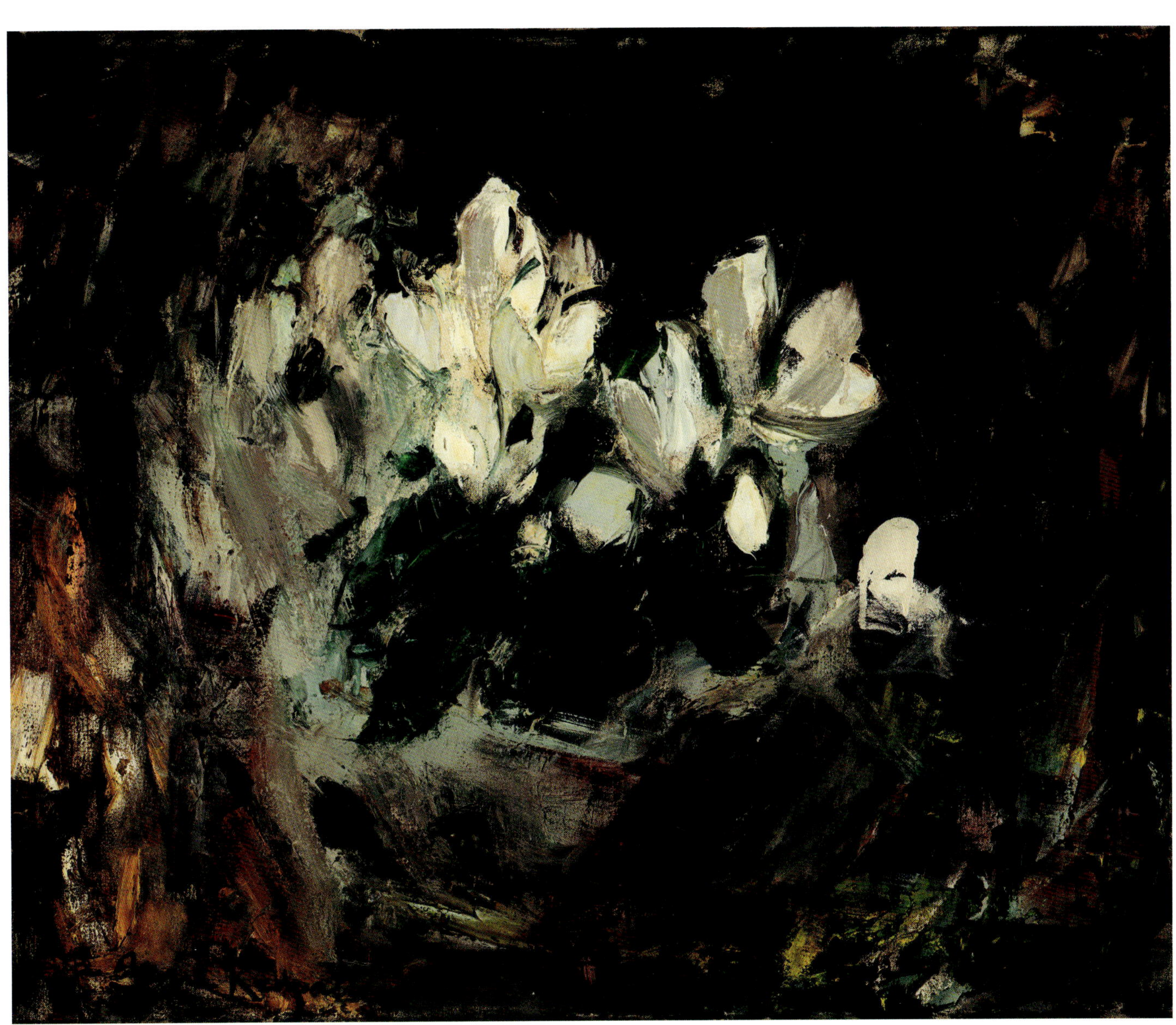

Henri Rousseau

1844–1910

A tightly packed bouquet of flowers bursts up out of a vase. The petals and leaves extend outwards, like fireworks, creating surprising clashes of colour. As in many of Henri Rousseau's works, there is a tension at the heart of *Bouquet of Flowers* between quiet stillness and wild movement. The painting is composed like a formal portrait, with the vase perfectly centred in the middle of the canvas. But despite the seeming stasis of the scene, the flowers are full of life and energy.

Bouquet of Flowers is one of several floral paintings that Rousseau made in the year leading up to his unexpected death in 1910 at the age of 66. While all the paintings have the same tabletop composition and curtained backdrop, each features a different arrangement of flowers. Several, including this one, contain forget-me-nots, selected perhaps for their commemorative meaning. Rousseau was sensitive to the emotional significance of flowers. In a double portrait of the poet Guillaume Apollinaire and painter Marie Laurencin, he chose to include a row of *l'œillet de poète* (Sweet William) for the flower's poetic name.

The other flowers in the bouquet are harder to identify. Vibrant and fantastical, they resemble the vegetation in the jungle scenes for which Rousseau is best known. The artist claimed to have served with the French army in Mexico, but in fact never left his homeland. The plant life he depicted was therefore entirely drawn from his imagination and his observations of tropical flora at the Jardin des Plantes in Paris. Of his visits the artist said: 'When I am in these hothouses and see the strange plants from exotic lands, it seems to me that I am entering a dream.' ***NP***

Bouquet of Flowers,
circa 1909–10
Oil on canvas
61 x 49.5 cm
Tate: Bequeathed by
C. Frank Stoop 1933

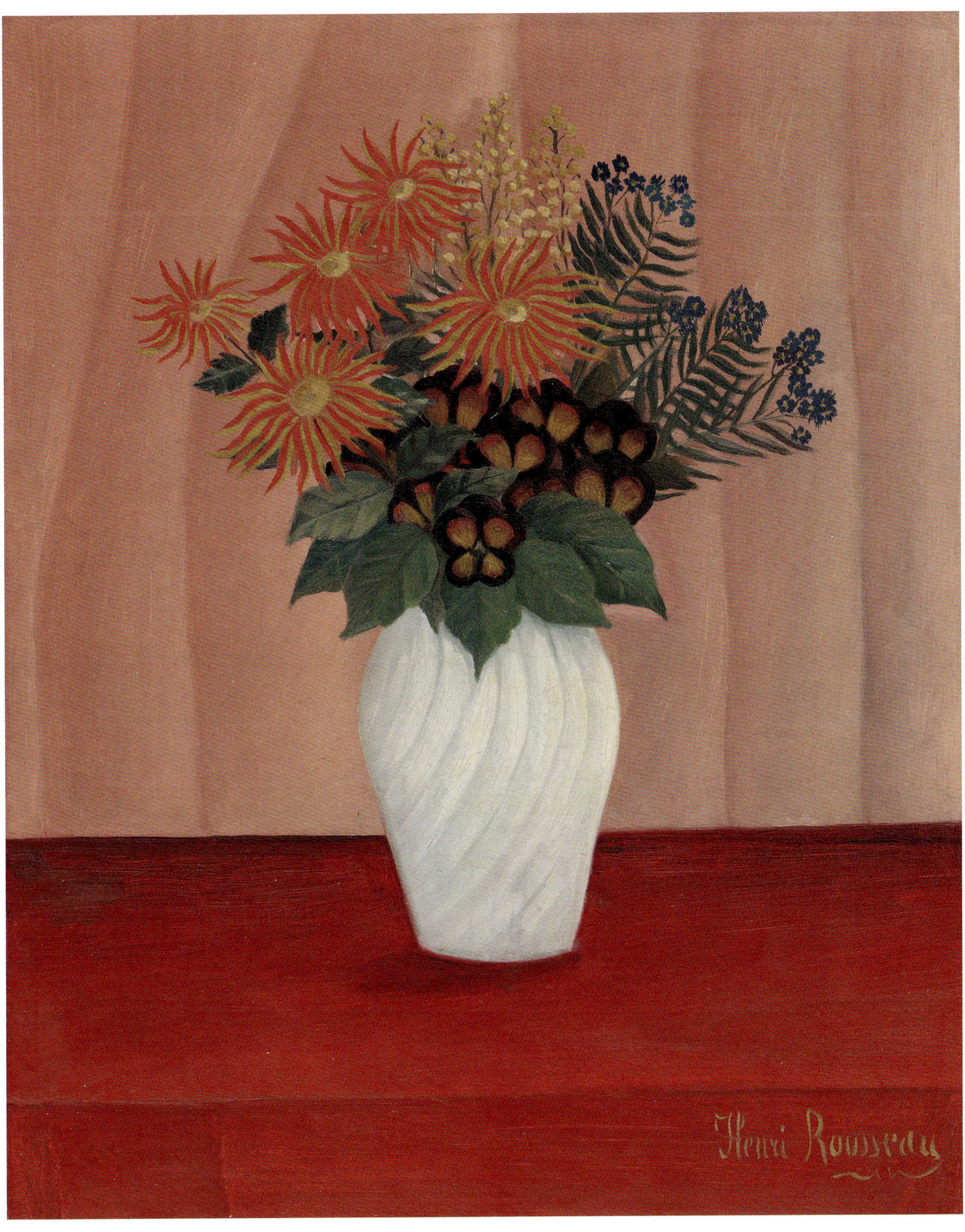
Henri Rousseau

William Scott

1913–1989

A warm golden hue surrounds a scattered assortment of yellow and orange flowers in William Scott's *Still Life–Flowers and Jug*. The spindly stems and intertwined leaves cause disruption to the otherwise ordered composition. While the jug stands on the table, ready to be used, the scene awaits a human presence. Scott's experimental rendering of flower painting does not depict a perfectly curated arrangement, but rather the state of disarray.

Created just after the Second World War, this painting exemplifies Scott's distinctive method of simplifying objects and exploring their potential to reveal the nature of human relationships. The kitchen table is a recurring motif in Scott's paintings from the 1940s, transforming in later works to a simple and abstract form. Scott used unremarkable everyday objects to experiment with colour and shape. His approach to representing the domestic was strongly influenced both by the reinvention of the still life genre in the early twentieth century, for example in the Cubist works of Pablo Picasso and Georges Braque, as well as the flattened architectural spaces depicted in early European art.

The amorphous cloth or paper on the table in this painting suggests that the flowers have just been unwrapped and will soon be placed in the jug beside them. However, the way in which they lie scattered across the table also foreshadows their inevitable wilting and decay. This creates a sense of uncertainty. At what point during the lifespan of these flowers has this scene been captured? Will the flowers be arranged and presented in a beautiful bouquet, or simply discarded? *MB*

Still Life–Flowers and Jug, 1946
Oil on canvas
73 x 83 cm
Lent by Birmingham Museums Trust on behalf of Birmingham City Council

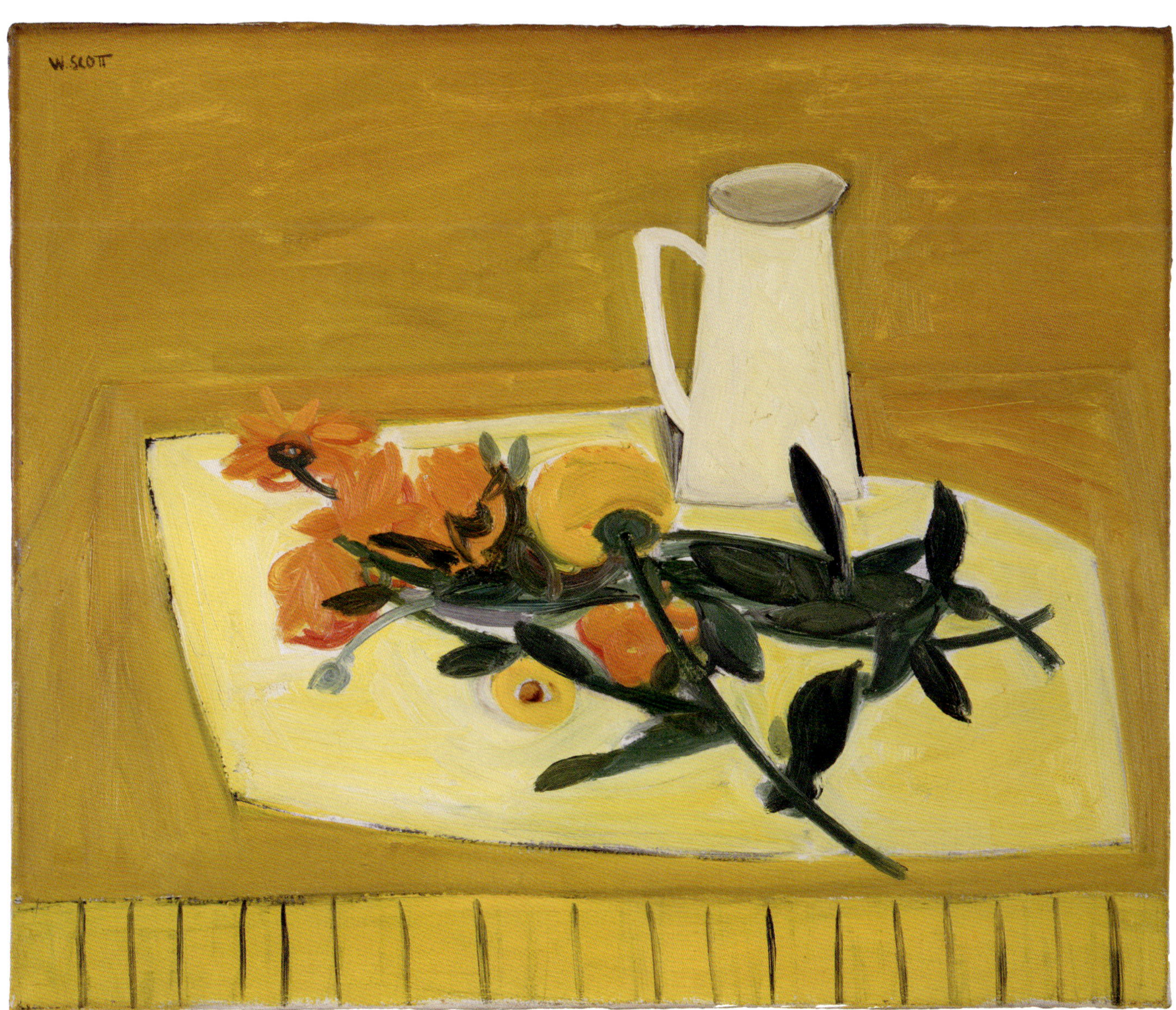
W. SCOTT

Judith Tucker

1960–2023

Windswept sea aster flowers are just about discernible in Judith Tucker's exuberant composition. The fragile white petals, in the process of turning into pappi, are nestled within a tangle of marshy leaves and stems that sprawls across the canvas. The painting has an elemental quality, combining different tidal states and times of night and day. The left side of the composition is stormy, wet and dark, while the right side is illuminated, green and dry.

This painting is from Tucker's *Dark Marsh* series, in which she depicted plants growing on the Tetney Marshes – an area on the Lincolnshire coast known for its salt marshes, mudflats and lagoons. It is part of *Hideaway*, a long-running collaborative project with the poet Harriet Tarlo, which combined paintings and poetry and featured in the artists' book *Saltwort*. In *Dark Marsh*, Tucker and Tarlo focused on plants that are vulnerable to rises in the sea level but which also help to protect the land from flooding. This dual process is evident in the composition of this painting: the plant is simultaneously being engulfed by waves and in the act of repelling them.

Tucker's method of painting involved a complex process of layering. She began by painting the entire canvas in a single colour and then covering it with a coat of aluminium powder, before building up layers of paint with stark tonal differences. She described her technique as a version of traditional *chiaroscuro*, a way of creating strong dramatic contrasts between light and shadow, popularised during the Renaissance. The effect is that the plants appear surreally real, glowing with a more-than-natural vibrancy. Her sea asters – perennial flowers that persist year after year – become a metaphor for cycles of life and death. ***NP***

Dark Marsh: Sea Aster, 2022
Oil on linen
60 x 80 cm
Private collection

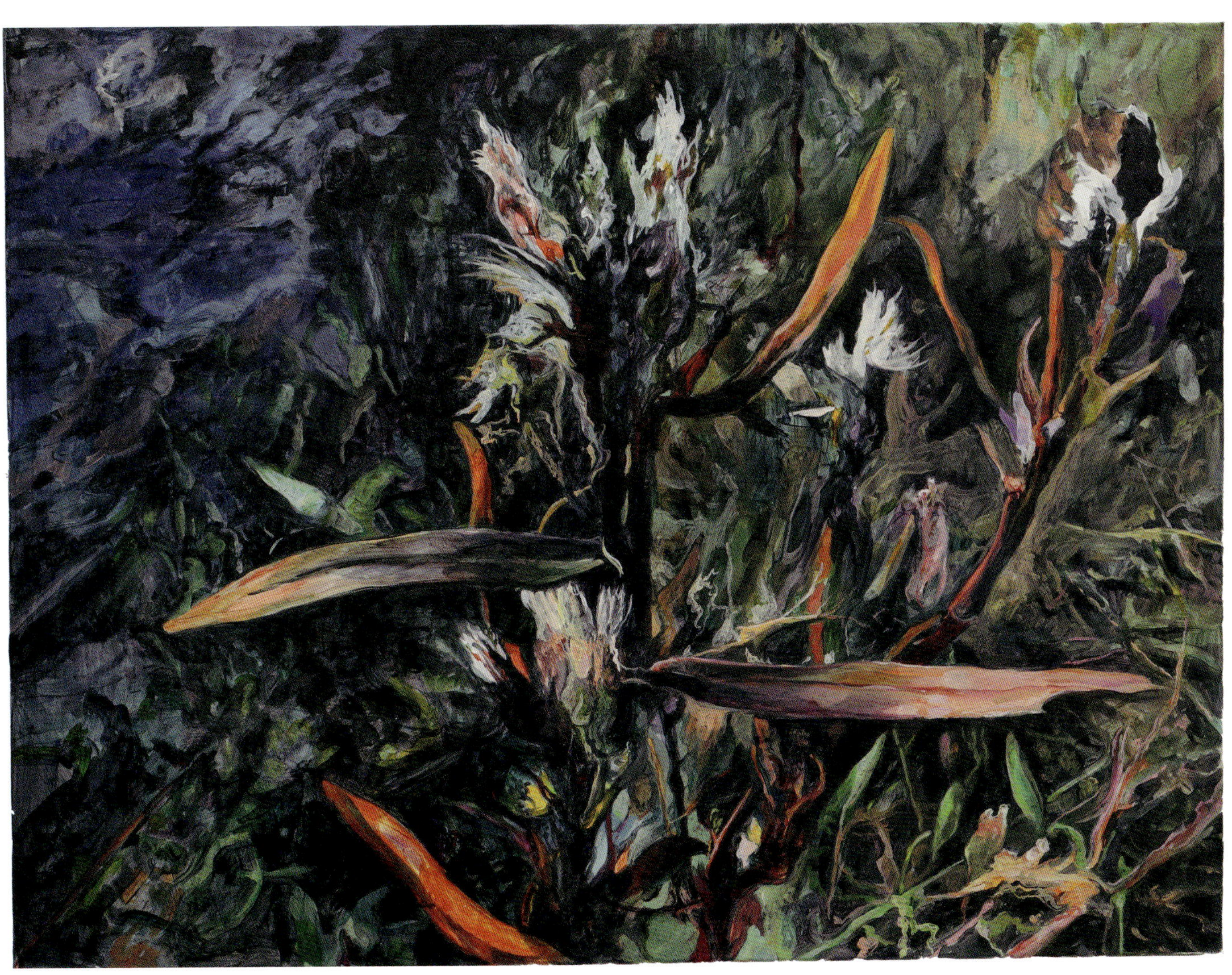

Euan Uglow

1932–2000

A small sprig of narcissus extends from a glass vase in Euan Uglow's delicate painting. The crisp white flowers sing against the radiant yellow background. Only the rim of the vase is visible, so that the focus of the painting is the singular stem of flowers, just handpicked. With the narcissus taking centre stage, the small vase that contains it appears to be a footnote within the composition.

Uglow's softly delineated flowers are contrasted with the rigorous mark making that was a key element of his painting process. The small dark crosses and lines on and around the flowers show the artist's method of implementing structure. Yet, despite the deliberate nature of their construction, the narcissus flowers appear fragile and beautiful. During the 1970s, Uglow simplified his still-life configurations and experimented with the relationships between the objects depicted. In this period he also started basing his compositions within a single colour, a compositional feature that is referenced in the title of this painting.

Uglow leaves room for the viewer's interpretation. The crosses marking out space, left by the artist in the finished painting, record the process of making, creating a sense of tension between past and present. Uglow was known to fix his still-life compositions in place, discouraging any hint of movement. In this painting, however, there is a suggestion of subtle motion. One flower appears to float on the canvas, slightly detached from the stem. Although only partially included, the vase is a clear, solid object, juxtaposed with the eerie, fragmented flowers. The contrast between the natural and man-made elements in the painting draws attention to the role of the artist and the artificiality of painting. *MB*

Narcissus on Yellow Background, 1978
Oil on canvas laid on panel
38.6 x 38.6 cm
De Beers Art Collection

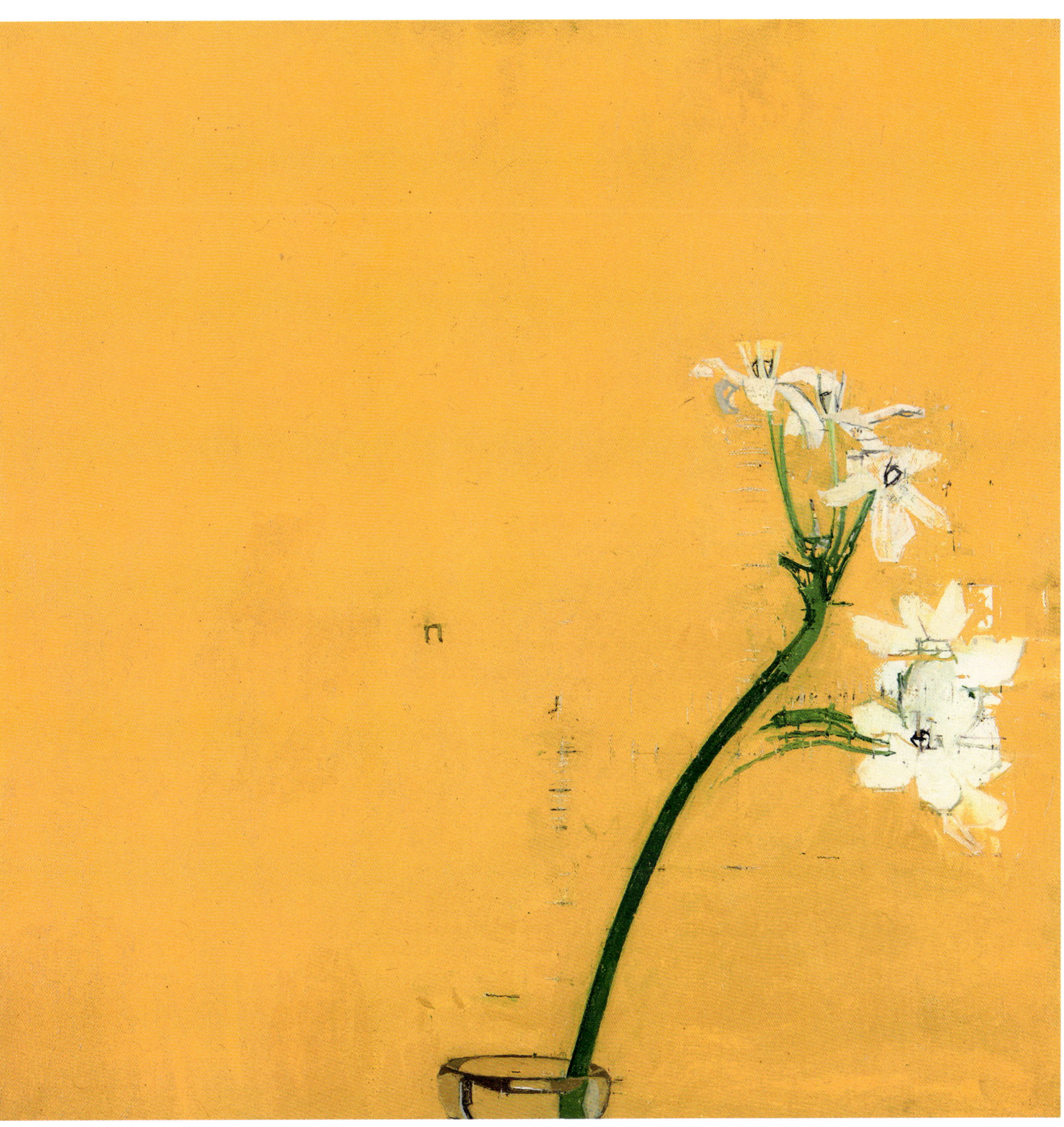

Charlotte Verity

Born 1954

Emerging through a blurry haze, a cluster of snowdrops droops and sways against the icy winter wind and rain. Charlotte Verity paints outside through the seasons, regardless of the weather, to observe and record the likeness of flowers. Her method of working *en plein air* creates a sense of spontaneity and energy. *In the Green* captures the snowdrops in motion, bouncing with every droplet of rain. Rather than creating botanical records, Verity depicts flowers in an inherently painterly way, conveying her sensitivity, knowledge and care towards the natural world.

Verity's depictions of flowers materialise from long periods of observation and study. Whatever she paints comes from her garden, until recently in urban south London and now in rural Somerset. When working in her studio, the artist opens the space to the elements, whether in the height of summer or the depths of winter, to experience the same natural environment as her subjects. Inspired by the charged atmospheres of artists John Constable and Gwen John, as well as the light-filled spaces of Renaissance painter Piero della Francesca, Verity looks to her art historical antecedents when capturing the quietness of nature. In her paintings, snowdrops and other wildflowers, fruit and foliage, exist only in light, almost like an apparition.

In the Green is not a typical flower painting. Unlike in many floral compositions, the snowdrops have not been situated within the studio or home, removed from their natural environment. They inhabit their own world, close to the earth and unarranged. Verity's notion of flower painting extends beyond the studio: rather than being positioned within a curated set of objects, the snowdrops are part of the landscape. Verity's work provokes meditations on the fragility of the natural world and our propensity to domesticate it. *MB*

In the Green, 2021
Oil on canvas
25.5 x 31 cm
Courtesy the artist

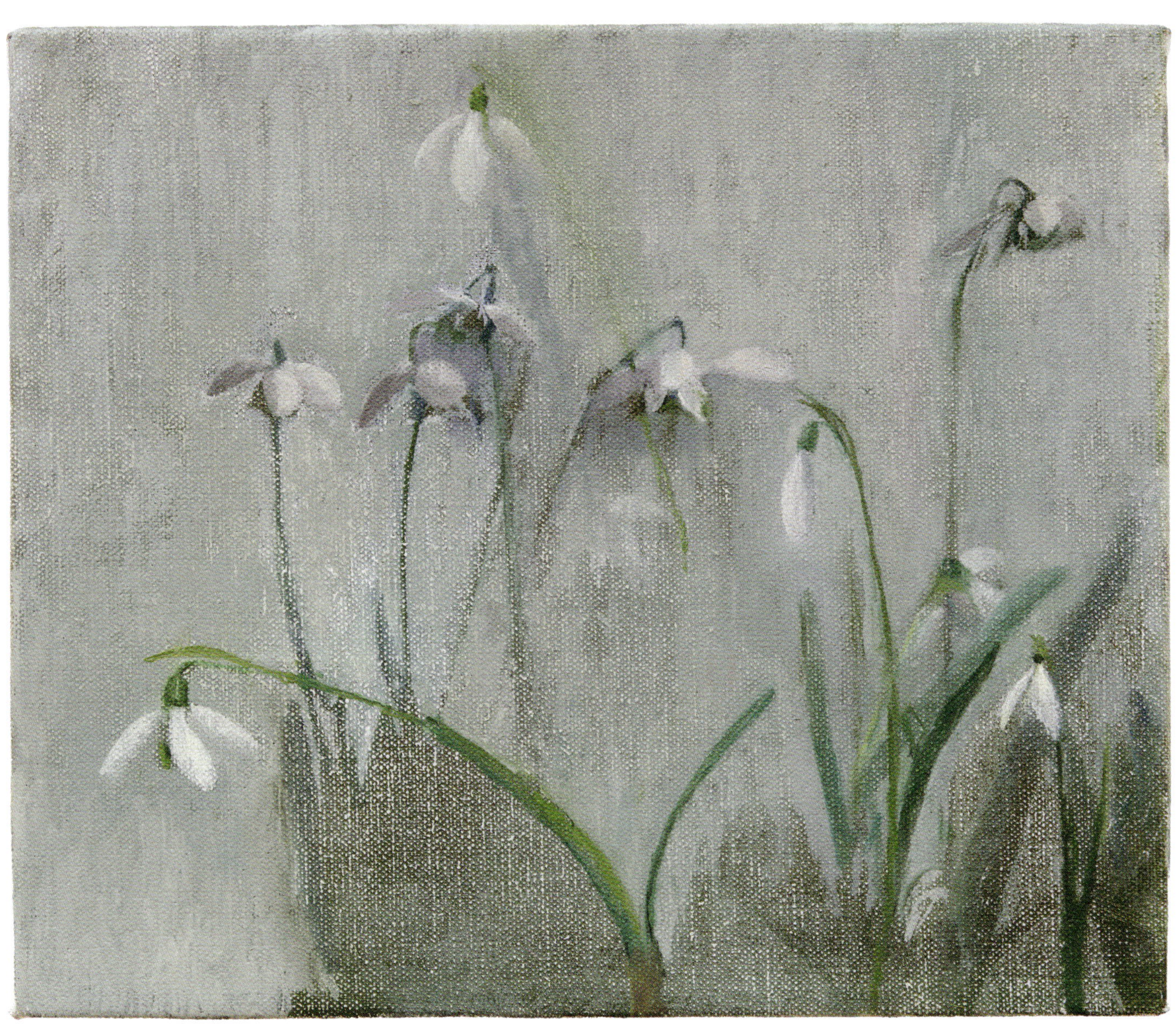

Édouard Vuillard

1868–1940

Emerging from a flurry of colour, an arrangement of wildflowers in a stoneware jug is the centrepiece of Édouard Vuillard's *Pot de grès et fleurs*. The artist's application of paint in small, energetic bursts remains consistent throughout the composition, resulting in an ambiguous sense of depth and space. However, with their vibrant white, yellow and green hues, the flowers stand out against the more muted lilac-grey tones of the background.

From the late 1880s, Vuillard was part of Les Nabis, an avant-garde art movement in Paris that pursued a simplified approach to composition, form and colour, as initiated by Post-Impressionist artists such as Paul Gauguin. However, from 1900 Vuillard adopted a form of naturalism that was more concerned with direct observation as a means of exploring interior light and space. Throughout his career, Vuillard's work was characterised by a focus on the interior, often in the form of introspective scenes of everyday domestic life. Many of his paintings depicted the small Paris apartments that he shared with his mother. This composition has a spontaneous air, like a snapshot of a room, rather than a considered arrangement set up specifically for the painting.

In *Pot de grès et fleurs*, the blooms and the jug that contains them, the table they are perched on, the painting hung on the wall and the other items of domestic ephemera all appear to merge with one another and fade in and out of focus. When painting ordinary, familiar objects Vuillard often chose unusual angles and compositions. The central position of the flowers within the composition grounds the viewer in an otherwise hazy, disorientating space. *MB*

Pot de grès et fleurs,
circa 1900–10
Oil on canvas
77.5 x 54 cm
Fitzwilliam Museum,
University of Cambridge

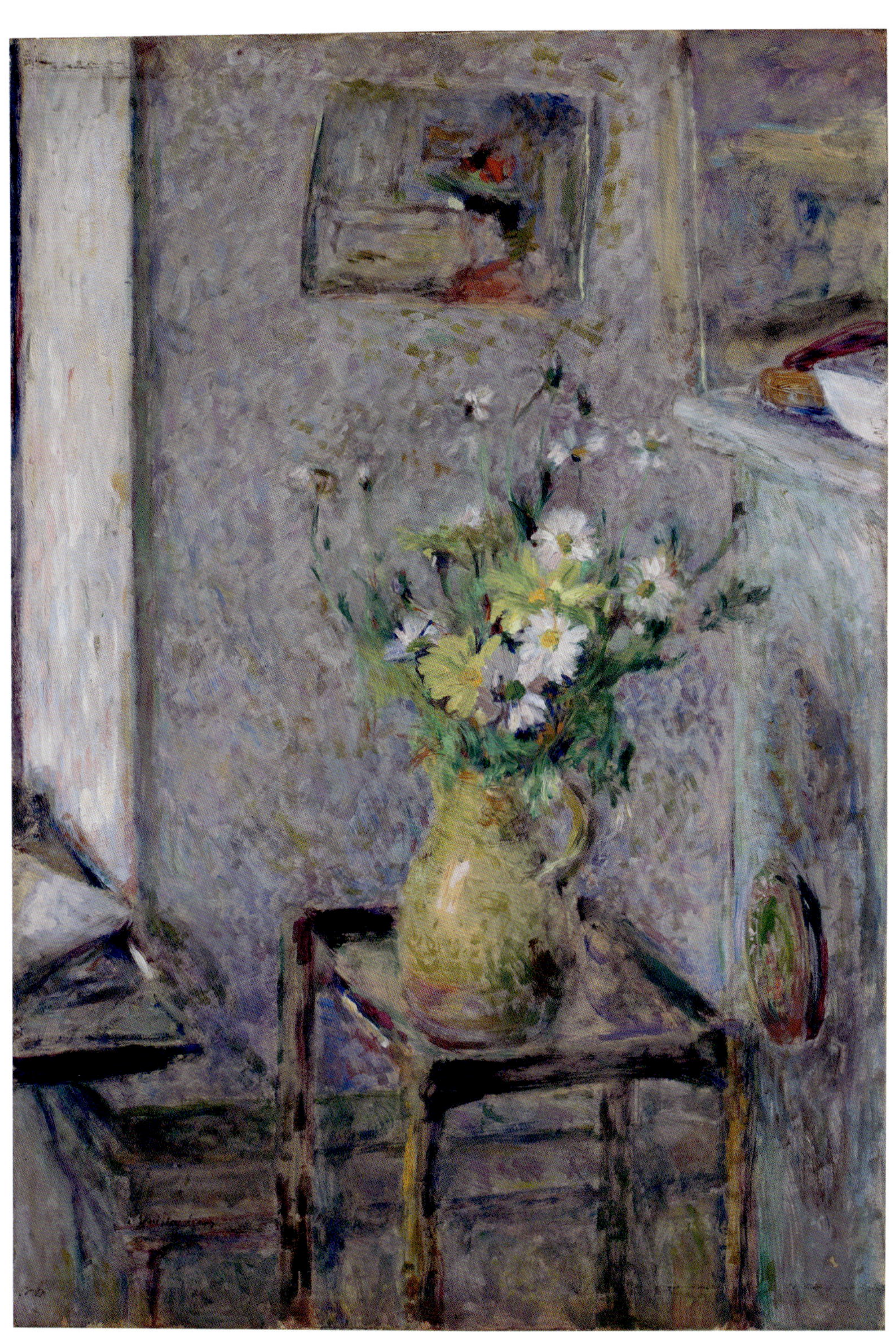

Caroline Walker

Born 1982

An ample bouquet of flowers is the centrepiece of Caroline Walker's painting *Kitchen Table*. The unfurled paper wrapping, half-open scissors and trimmings of stems and leaves suggest that the flowers have only just been arranged in the vase, with the mess created by the task still waiting to be tidied up. In the background the artist's daughter, Daphne, is shown drawing with felt-tip pens. The artist herself is the invisible presence in the composition, performing the simultaneous roles of caregiver, flower-arranger and observer.

Throughout her artistic career, Walker has represented women's labour, both in the workplace and in the home. Over the last few years, she has focused in particular on women's experiences of domesticity and motherhood, portraying aspects of daily life that are often forgotten or overlooked. In Walker's paintings, seemingly innocuous objects – laundry baskets, laptops, breast pumps and water bottles – are charged with symbolic and emotional meaning. Flowers appear periodically in these works. In *Deliveries* (2022), for example, Walker portrays a tableful of flower bouquets and other presents which she describes as 'the well-meaning gifts that arrive when you are in the early days with a baby'.

Walker uses her own photographs as the starting point for each painting. In this composition, she frames the kitchen table as the site for multiple everyday activities. Each object points to a different function: the sheets of paper and box of felt-tip pens, the placemats, the baby's 'sippy cup', the ceramic candle holder. With their inherently short lifespan, the flowers become emblematic of the shifting, transitory uses of the table. However, Walker's painting preserves the flowers in time, conferring the act of their arrangement at the kitchen table with importance and permanence. ***NP***

Kitchen Table, 2025
Oil on linen
99 x 75 cm
Courtesy the artist; GRIMM, Amsterdam/New York/London; and Ingleby Gallery, Edinburgh

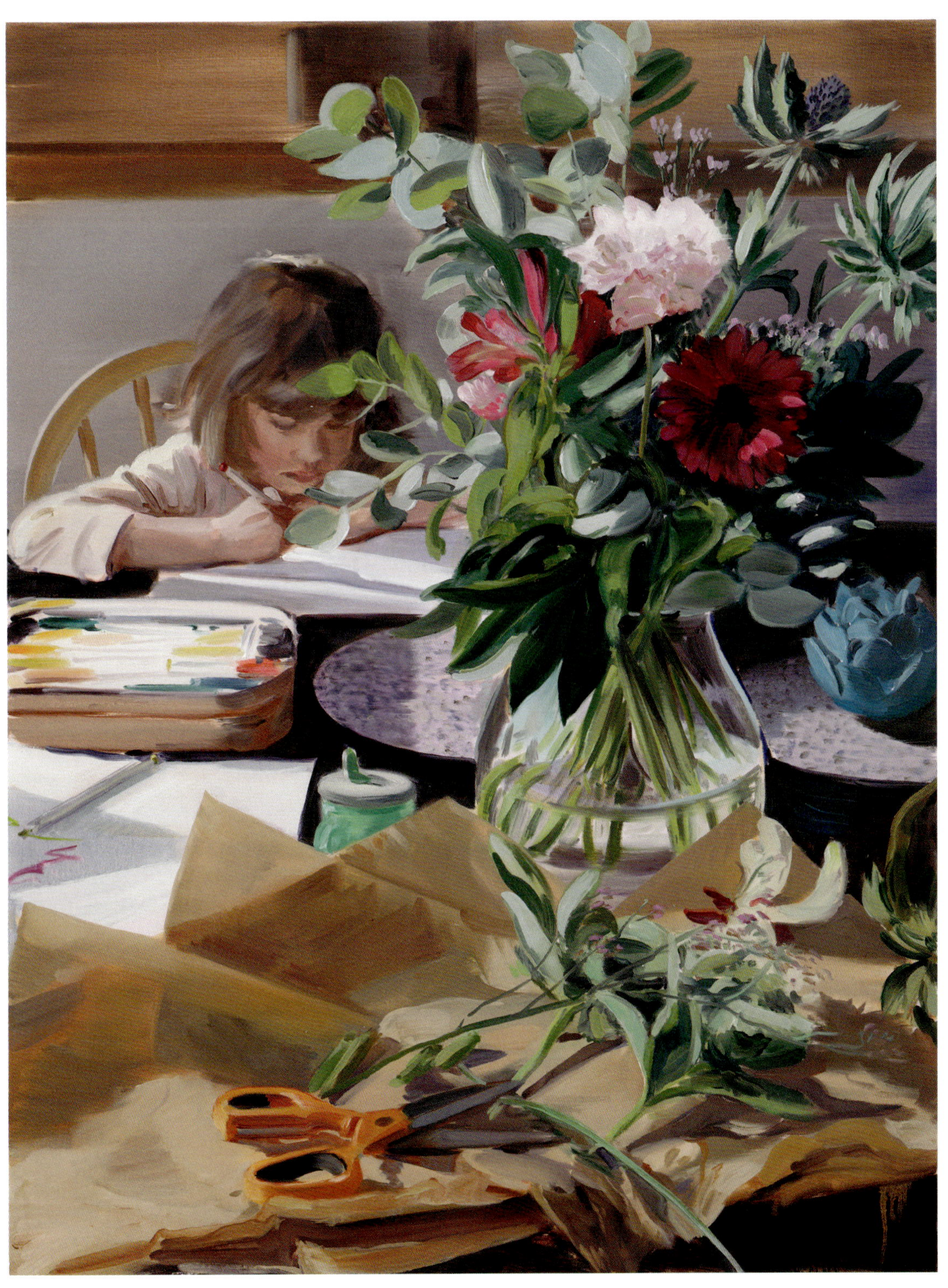

Alison Watt

Born 1965

A stem with three rose heads rests on an indeterminate light blue-grey surface in Alison Watt's *Lying Down*. The flower casts a dramatic shadow onto the pale expanse, as though it were being viewed under a raking light. The creamy pink petals of the rose are just beginning to wilt and take on an amber-brown hue. 'As soon as a rose is picked, it's dying,' the artist has said. She captures roses at different stages of bloom and decay within their short lifespan.

Watt started painting flowers in the late 2010s while studying the work of the portraitist Allan Ramsay. She was particularly drawn to Ramsay's painting of his young wife Margaret Lindsay of Evelick, whom he pictured in the act of arranging flowers. Watt created a series of flower paintings titled after Margaret Lindsay Ramsay in which the rose she holds in her portrait is isolated and magnified. Having begun her artistic career with portraits too, in the 1990s Watt turned to painting objects – draped fabric, pieces of paper, books and feathers – which implied a human presence without including any figures. Her paintings of roses point not just to the person who has picked or arranged the flowers, but to a romantic intimacy shared by two people.

The title of *Lying Down* suggests that the rose itself has chosen its recumbent pose. However, with the picked end of the stem in the lower foreground, the flower's placement subtly implicates the viewer in the scene. Within the large expanse of the canvas, the rose remains within touching distance. Larger-than-life and glowing radiantly, the rose has a seductive presence – an invitation for the viewer to look, and carry on looking. *NP*

Lying Down, 2025
Oil on canvas
122 x 102 cm
Courtesy Lévy Gorvy Dayan

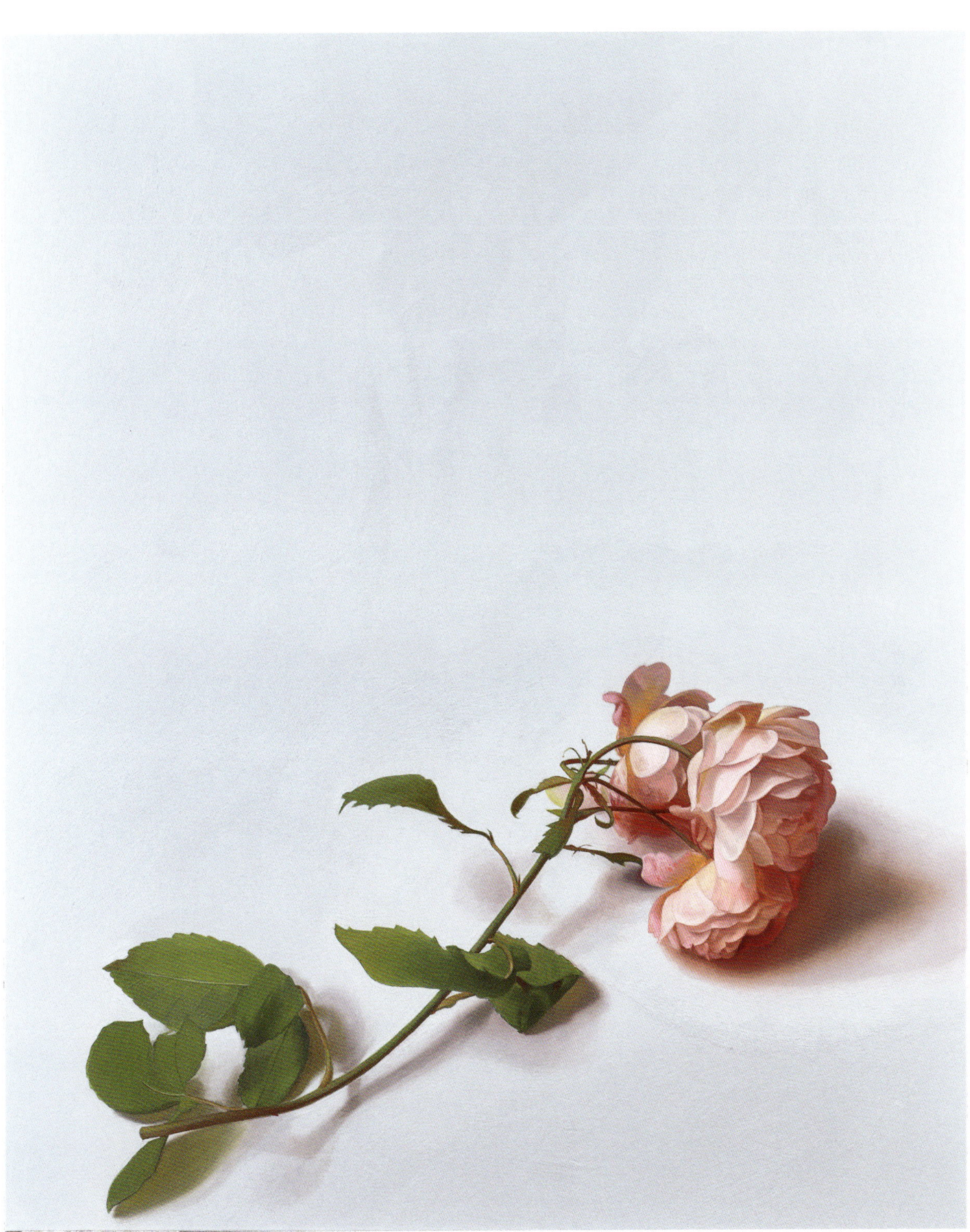

Christopher Wood
1901–1930

From an encroaching darkness, Christopher Wood depicts flowers bursting from a white vase, like a beacon of light. The bouquet is composed of juxtapositions of colour and form. Bright red and white tulips with their crisp, pointed petals cut through the muted, earthy greens of the surrounding foliage. Large foreboding dark green leaves envelop small, soft yellow and purple flowers. Painted during the last year of Wood's tragically short life, *The White Vase* possesses a sense of poignant turbulence.

Wood's paintings of flowers were often experimental studies in colour and form or homages to his artistic influences. Wood was a self-taught artist and he strove to emulate the fresh and direct approach to painting of artists such as Henri Rousseau, Alfred Wallis and Vincent van Gogh. The influence of Van Gogh is evident in *The White Vase*, where Wood employs a similar frontal perspective to that in the Dutch artist's compositions, most famously his depictions of sunflowers. A flattened appearance to both the flowers and the white vase can also be seen in Rousseau's *Bouquet of Flowers*, also painted during the last year of the artist's life.

Nature and rural life became an obsession for Wood, stemming from his ambition to be a successful modern painter. He believed that the simplicity of Van Gogh's rustic existence in the South of France was fundamental to the artist's approach to art and life. Wood experienced rural life himself while staying with his artist friends Ben and Winifred Nicholson at their home in Bankshead in Cumberland (now Cumbria) in the spring of 1928 – a pivotal moment for Wood artistically. Nature therefore became a source of refuge for Wood. Winifred Nicholson regularly sent cut flowers to Wood when he was living in Paris, providing souvenirs of way of the life he craved. ***MB***

The White Vase, 1930
Oil on canvas on board
46 x 38 cm
Pallant House Gallery, Chichester (Bequeathed by Ian Mylles with Art Fund support 2021)

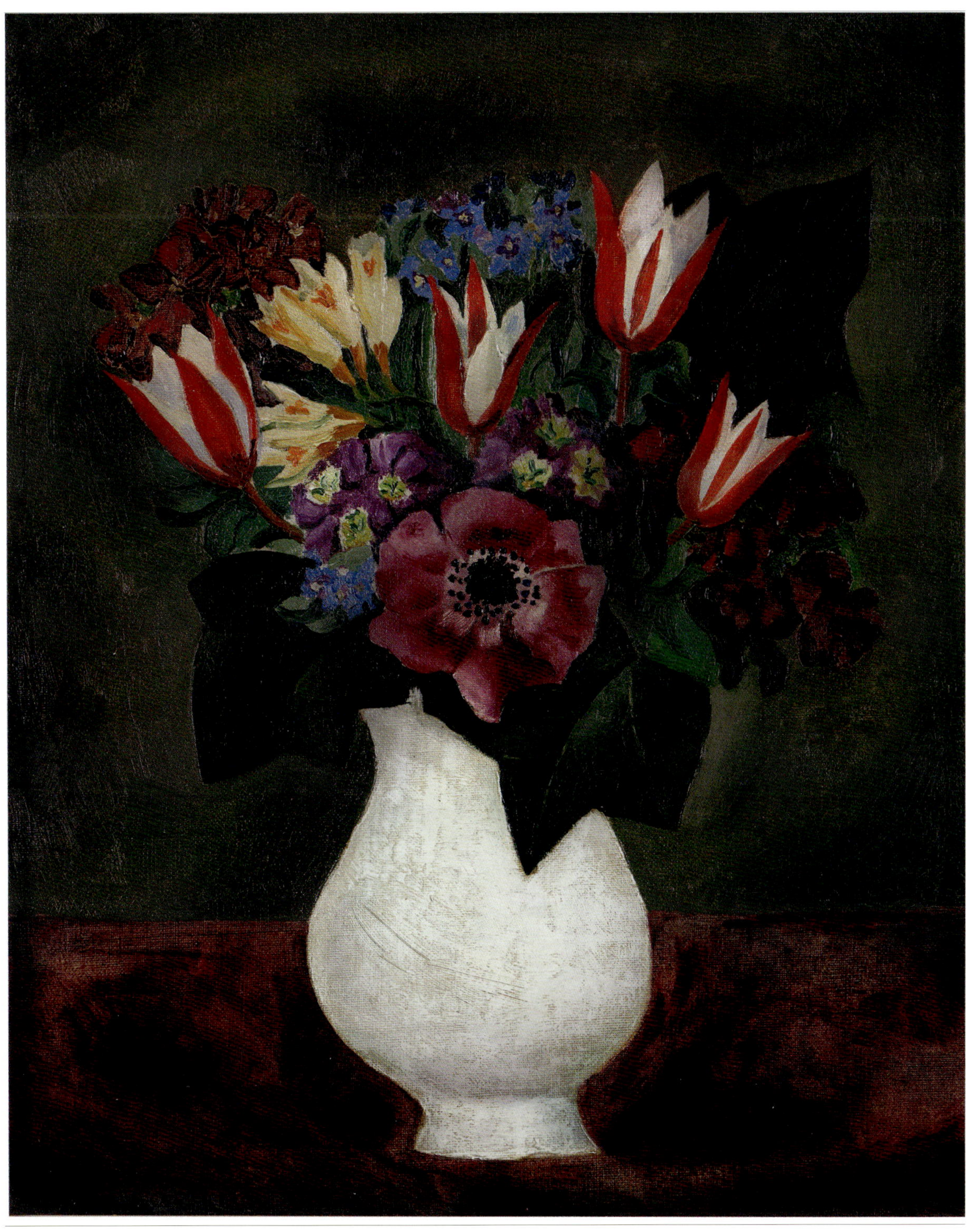

Clare Woods

Born 1972

An arrangement of flowers is conjured from murky pinks, acid greens and amber browns in Clare Woods' striking painting. The artist completes all her works in one session. She lays a sheet of aluminium flat on a trestle table and stands over it while applying her energetic brushstrokes, often using her whole body to move paint around the surface. The resulting works combine artistic control with a sense of freedom and unpredictability.

Woods was originally inspired to paint flowers by the series of sixteen floral works which Édouard Manet made on his deathbed as he died of syphilis. In 2020, when she herself was bedbound while recovering from a major surgery, she began to photograph the bouquets of flowers sent by her friends and family and later adapt them into paintings. 'I want flowers to look dead', she has said. She depicts flowers just past their bloom, as they start to gently rot and decay, stilled in a moment between life and death. Like in traditional still-life paintings, with their *memento mori*, her flowers symbolise the shortness of human life.

Sweet Hill is based on photographs taken in the Kettle's Yard house, capturing a vase of flowers in Helen Ede's bedroom where she too spent periods of convalescence. The title is a reference to Honey Hill, which can be seen from the bedroom window. This setting is not evident in the painting itself, however, as the background is obscured by washes of dark colour. Painted in putrid green, the container of the floral arrangement subtly conflates the stems of flowers with the glass of the vase. The bouquet therefore dominates the composition, permeating it with its larger-than-life scale and surreal colour. Woods transforms the delicate vase of natural garden flowers into a lurid spectacle, suffused with emotional intensity and deathly foreboding. ***NP***

Sweet Hill, 2026
Oil on aluminium
70 x 50 cm
Courtesy the artist

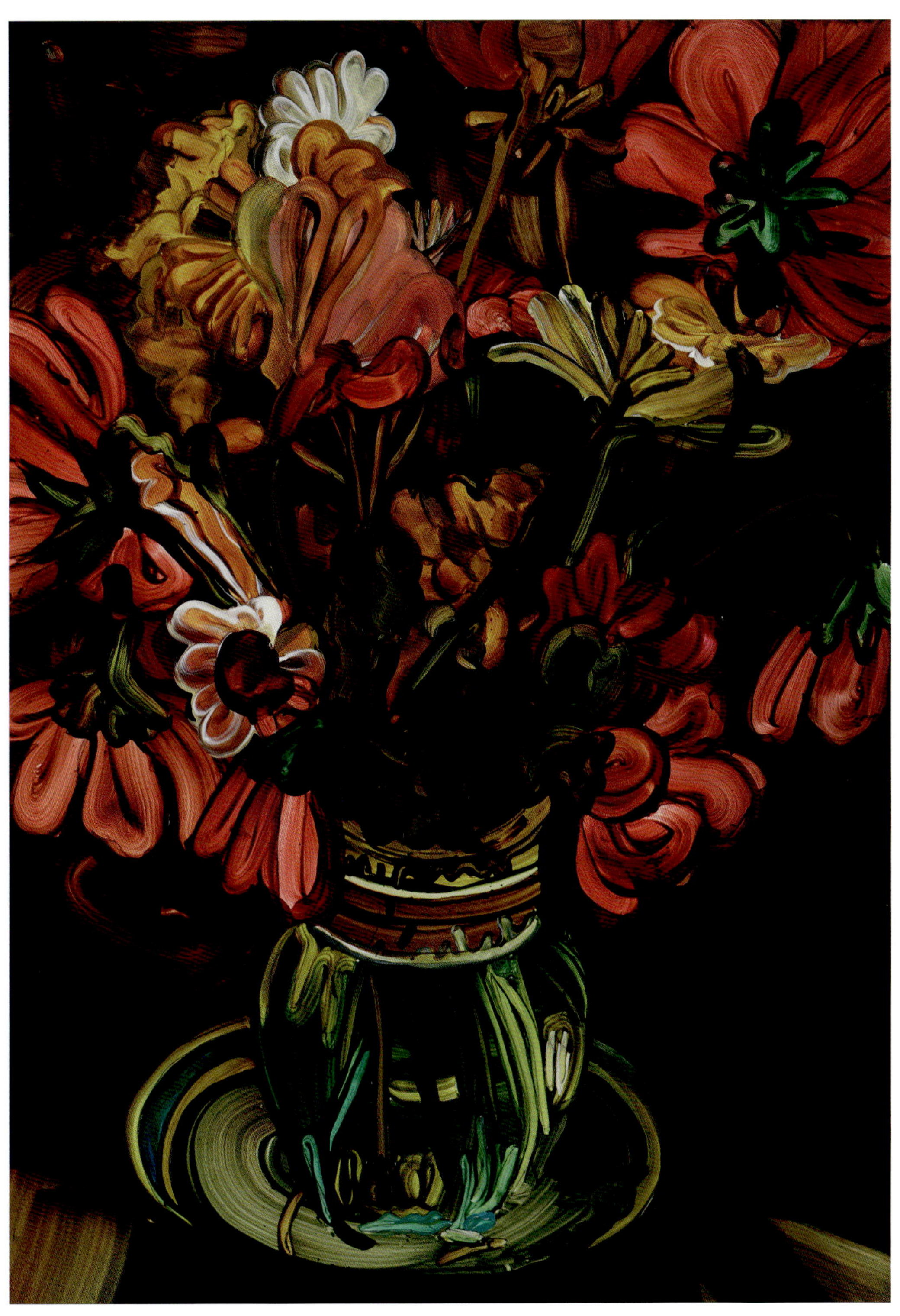

Artist Biographies

Hurvin Anderson born 1965 graduated with a BA from Wimbledon School of Art (1994) and an MA in Painting from the Royal College of Art (1998). His vivid landscapes and interiors, often based on his own photography and memories, explore the themes of diaspora and belonging. In March 2026, a major retrospective of his work opened at Tate Britain.

Vanessa Bell 1879-1961 was a founding member of the Bloomsbury Group, an influential circle of artists, writers and intellectuals in the first three decades of the twentieth century. Bell herself was a pioneering artist whose early Modernist work was featured in *The Second Post-Impressionist Exhibition* in 1912. As well as painting, Bell designed textiles, ceramics and interiors and was a co-director of the Omega Workshops with fellow artists Roger Fry and Duncan Grant between 1913 and 1919.

David Bomberg 1890-1957 was a British painter and one of the Whitechapel Boys, a group of young, Jewish artists influential in British Modernism. After being expelled from the Slade School of Fine Art for his radical approach, he exhibited with the Camden Town Group (1913) and London Group (1914). He abandoned his Futurist aesthetic following the First World War, instead turning to portraits of friends and dramatic landscapes.

Louise Bourgeois 1911-2010 was born in Paris and, as a young artist, engaged with Existentialism and Surrealism, encouraged by Joan Miró and Fernand Léger. In 1938, she settled in New York. Her work, spanning sculpture, installation, painting, drawing and prints, was largely underappreciated until it was recognised by a new generation of women artists in the 1970s, many of whom Bourgeois mentored. She gained further prominence after a 1982 retrospective of her work at the Museum of Modern Art in New York. In 2001, she was the first artist commissioned to exhibit in Tate Modern's Turbine Hall.

Jai Chuhan born 1955 is an Indian-born British painter who studied at the Slade School of Fine Art. Her paintings depict vividly coloured abstracted interiors inhabited by female figures. In 2024, Chuhan was shortlisted for the David and Yuko Juda Art Foundation Grant, curated by Peter Doig, and her work featured in the Hayward touring exhibition *Acts of Creation: On Art and Motherhood*, curated by Hettie Judah (2024-25). Her paintings have been included in solo and group exhibitions at museums and galleries including Tate Liverpool; Barbican Art Gallery, London; Ikon, Birmingham; and art fairs including Art Basel with the Approach, London; Frieze London, Art Mumbai; and India Art Fair with Vadehra Art Gallery, New Delhi.

Andrew Cranston born 1969 is a Scottish artist known for his paintings of domestic worlds, ranging in size from linen-bound book covers to large-scale canvases. In 1996, he graduated with an MA in Painting from the Royal College of Art, where he was tutored by painters Peter Doig and Adrian Berg. His first institutional solo exhibition was held at the Hepworth Wakefield in 2023.

Kaye Donachie born 1970 received a Fine Art degree from the University of Central England, Birmingham (1992), and a MA in Painting from the Royal College of Art (1997). Her paintings draw on both archival and personal imagery to create dreamlike narratives that often centre on the lives and legacies of marginalised women. Solo exhibitions include those at Le Plateau Frac Île-de-France, Paris (2017), Lismore Castle, County Waterford, Ireland (2021) and Pallant House Gallery, Chichester (2023).

Gigi Ettedgui born 1992 is a British painter who moved to Florence in 2020 to study classical oil painting at the Charles Cecil Studio. Before this, she lived and worked in Paris, assisting the Creative Director of Hermès. In 2024, she returned to London to work in a studio space in St Paul's Studios, where she produces paintings of flowers from life in natural lighting.

Anna Freeman Bentley born 1982 received her BA from Chelsea College of Art and Design in 2004 and her MA from the Royal College of Art in 2010. Her depictions of interiors, ranging from staged domestic spaces to junk shops, restaurants and private members clubs, are influenced by the ideas and architecture of the Baroque. Selected solo exhibitions include Anat Ebgi, LA (2024), MassimodeCarlo Pièce Unique, Paris (2024) and Frestonian Gallery, London (2022).

Marjory Garnett 1897-1977 was born in Windermere and over the course of several decades went on expeditions to the Arctic, where she observed and recorded the plants and birds of the region. Her work is held in the collections of the Polar Museum at Scott Polar Research Institute, Cambridge, and Tullie House Museum and Art Gallery, Carlisle.

Tirzah Garwood 1908-1950 was a British painter, wood-engraver and paper marbler, who was married to the artist Eric Ravilious. She studied at the Eastbourne School of Art where she was introduced to wood-engraving in 1926. Her work was first exhibited by the Society of Wood Engravers the following year and she later undertook illustrative commissions for the Kynoch Press and BBC. In 1931, Garwood and Ravilious moved to Essex and became members of the Great Bardfield Artists group. In 1944, she began producing oil paintings of natural scenes, continuing until her death in 1950.

Gluck 1895-1978, born Hannah Gluckstein, joined the Lamorna artists' colony, near Penzance, in 1916. Here she adopted a masculine appearance and produced portraits and floral paintings. Refusing to identify with any artistic school or movement, Gluck displayed work only in solo exhibitions. For an exhibition at The Fine Art Society in 1932, Gluck developed patented three-tier wooden frames to integrate the artwork with the wall. She returned to the gallery in 1973 for a final exhibition of new work after a 30-year hiatus.

Lubaina Himid born 1954 was one of the leading figures of the British Black Art Movement in the 1980s, she often employs theatricality, pattern and colour to challenge dominant cultural narratives. Himid won the 2017 Turner Prize and the 2023 Maria Lassnig Prize. Her exhibition *Another Chance Encounter*, created in collaboration with Magda Stawarska, took place at Kettle's Yard in 2025. She was selected to represent the UK at the 2026 Venice Biennale.

Howard Hodgkin 1932-2017 was a Turner Prize-winning painter and printmaker, known for his expressive brushstrokes and colours. Born in London, Hodgkin was evacuated to New York during the Second World War where he found inspiration in works by Henri Matisse and Édouard Vuillard at the Museum of Modern Art. He did not identify with any schools or groups, instead drawing on a range of cultural influences. In 1984, he represented Great Britain at the Venice Biennale.

Isak of Igdlorpait 1866-1903 was a Greenlandic artist who documented everyday life in Igdlorpait (southwest Greenland) at the turn of the twentieth century. After losing his right arm in a hunting accident, he was hired as a shepherd and received paper and paints as payment for his work. Isak is said to have been a prolific illustrator, but only three of his sketchbooks are known to still exist.

Nerys Johnson 1942-2001 was an artist and curator. She studied Fine Art at Durham University and stayed in the northeast, working as Keeper of Fine Arts at Laing Art Gallery, Newcastle upon Tyne, from 1967 and Keeper in Charge at the Durham Light Infantry Museum and Arts Centre from 1970. After retiring in 1989, she concentrated on painting. Aged two, Johnson was diagnosed with rheumatoid arthritis, a chronic illness that led her to create increasingly small paintings, often depicting flowers or landscapes.

David Jones 1895-1974 was a British painter and Modernist poet. He was associated with artists and craftsmen in Sussex and Wales in the 1920s, working as an engraver and printer, while at the same time writing poetry and essays. In 1927 he met Jim Ede, who introduced him to critics, collectors and artists, and the following year he joined the Seven and Five Society. In 1937, he published *In Parenthesis*, an epic poem inspired by his experience as an infantryman in the First World War.

Poppy Jones born 1985 received her BA in Fine Art from Falmouth College of Art in 2007 before completing an MA in Fine Art Printmaking at the Royal College of Art, in 2010. She lives and works in Bexhill-on-Sea, creating reflective still lifes through a process of monotype printing and overpainting. Her first institutional solo exhibition in the UK opened at Towner Eastbourne in March 2026.

Joy Labinjo born 1994 received her BFA degree from Newcastle University in 2017 and MFA from the Ruskin School of Art in 2020. Labinjo's work is often large-scale and figurative, based on photographs of family, friends and historical figures. Her works have been displayed in solo exhibitions at Baltic Centre for Contemporary Art, Newcastle upon Tyne (2019), Southwark Park Gallery (2024) and Wolverhampton Art Gallery (2026). In 2021, she was commissioned by Art on the Underground to create a public artwork in Brixton Underground Station.

Doron Langberg born 1985 lives and works in New York City and is known for intimate paintings of subjects from queer love to sweeping landscapes. In 2012, they received an MFA from Yale University School of Art. Solo exhibitions of their work have taken place at Rubell Museum, Miami (2022), and Kunsthal, Rotterdam (2024). Langberg has been situated as part of 'New Queer Intimism', a loosely associated group of LGBTQ+ painters including Salman Toor and Louis Fratino.

Aubrey Levinthal born 1986 lives and works in Philadelphia. She completed her BA at the Pennsylvania State University (2008) and her MFA at Pennsylvania Academy of the Fine Arts (2011). Her paintings, often featuring the daily lives of characters in downtown Philadelphia, have been exhibited at the ICA, Boston, and the Flag Art Foundation, New York.

Charles Rennie Mackintosh 1868–1928 was a major figure of the Art Nouveau movement. As an architect in his native Scotland, he created designs for major buildings including the Herald Building (1894) and Glasgow School of Art (1896). His style garnered acclaim in Germany and Austria, where he contributed to the 8th Vienna Secession in 1900. In 1914, he moved to the Suffolk village of Walberswick, producing watercolour paintings of flowers from a fishing shed.

Rory McEwen 1932–1982 was a Scottish painter, musician, sculptor and television presenter. He was a prominent figure in the 1960s folk music revival movement and presented the folk and blues TV programme, *Hullaballoo*. From 1964, McEwen devoted himself to visual art, working with a wide range of materials including Perspex and glass. He is best known for his watercolour paintings on vellum.

Cedric Morris 1889–1982 was an artist and plantsman who settled in East Anglia after periods living in Cornwall, Paris and London, where he maintained a close friendship with Christopher Wood. He moved to rural Suffolk in 1929 with his partner, the painter Arthur Lett-Haines, to pursue both painting and horticulture. Morris and Lett-Haines opened the East Anglian School of Painting and Drawing in 1937, which was attended by artists including Lucian Freud and Maggi Hambling.

Cassi Namoda born 1988 Her paintings draw on art history, vernacular photography and film to reference narratives of post-colonial Africa. In 2024 she presented her first institutional exhibition at the Norval Foundation in Cape Town, South Africa. The following year, she was the recipient of the inaugural Sunley Window commission at Turner Contemporary, Margate, and her work was featured in the 16th Sharjah Biennale, UAE.

Mary Newcomb 1922-2008 began painting after moving to rural Norfolk in 1950, taking inspiration from her natural surroundings. She had previously studied Natural Sciences at Reading University and taught science and mathematics. Her first solo exhibition was held at Crane Kalman Gallery in 1970 and she continued to exhibit regularly at the gallery and nationally, including a touring retrospective in 1996.

William Nicholson 1872-1949 began his career in graphic design, working on posters and illustrations in collaboration with his brother-in-law James Pryde under the pseudonym 'The Beggarstaffs'. His focus shifted to painting after he began exhibiting at the International Society from 1898, encouraged by its President, the artist James McNeill Whistler. Despite being known for portraits of prominent British figures during his lifetime, his main devotion was landscape and still-life painting.

Winifred Nicholson 1893-1981 studied in London and Paris before marrying artist Ben Nicholson in 1920. Together they exhibited widely in the 1920s and in 1925 she became a member of the Seven and Five Society. Following their separation, she moved to Paris where she encountered Piet Mondrian and Wassily Kandinsky and her work became more abstract. In 1937, under the name Winifred Dacre, Nicholson contributed to the influential book *Circle: International Survey of Constructive Art*. She settled in Cumberland (now Cumbria) following the Second World War.

Chris Ofili born 1968 received his BFA from Chelsea College of Art in 1991 and MFA from the Royal College of Art in 1993. His work has been the subject of solo exhibitions at museums including the National Gallery, Tate Britain, and the Serpentine, London; the New Museum and Studio Museum in Harlem, New York; the Arts Club of Chicago; and Kestner Gesellschaft, Hanover. He won the Turner Prize in 1998 and represented Great Britain at the 50th Venice Biennale in 2003.

Jennifer Packer born 1984 is an American artist who received her BFA from Tyler University School of Art at Temple University in 2007, and her MFA from Yale School of Art in 2012. The largest survey of her work to date, *Jennifer Packer: The Eye is Not Satisfied with Seeing*, was presented at the Serpentine, London (2020) and the Whitney Museum of American Art, New York (2021-22). She is Assistant Professor of Painting at the Rhode Island School of Design.

Celia Paul born 1959 lives and works in London, where she attended the Slade School of Fine Art between 1976 and 1981. Paul paints portraits of people close to her, especially her mother and four sisters, in addition to landscapes and still lifes. Her recent solo exhibitions include *Innervisions*, Gladstone Gallery, New York, 2026; *Celia Paul: Water Divining*, Sant' Andrea de Scaphis, Rome, and *Colony of Ghosts*, Victoria Miro, London, both in 2025. In 2018, Hilton Als curated a solo exhibition of Paul's work at the Yale Center for British Art in New Haven, Connecticut. Paul is the author of *Self Portrait* and *Letters to Gwen John*, a series of letters addressed to Paul's tutelary spirit. In 2012, Pallant House Gallery, Chichester, held an exhibition of the two artists' work, titled *Gwen John and Celia Paul: Painters in Parallel*.

Bryan Pearce 1927-2007 was a Cornish painter known for his portrayals of the St Ives landscape. Born with a rare condition affecting brain development, he was encouraged to start painting by his mother, who was an artist herself, and other St Ives artists. He studied at Leonard Fuller's St Ives School of Painting and later joined the Penwith Society (1957) and Newlyn Society (1959). His first solo exhibition was at Newlyn Gallery in 1959 and he quickly gained national popularity for his paintings of daily life in Cornwall.

Emma Prempeh born 1996 is a British artist with Ghanaian and Vincentian heritage. She completed a BA in Fine Art at Goldsmiths, University of London, in 2019 and an MA in Painting at the Royal College of Art, in 2022. She is known for her large-scale canvases using Schlag metal, which oxidises over time, slowly animating the painting. Her work has been exhibited as part of Bloomberg New Contemporaries (2019) and at Walker Art Gallery, Liverpool (2024).

Bianca Raffaella born 1992 is a British artist and activist who creates floral and figurative works. She became the first registered blind student to graduate from Kingston University in Visual Art in 2016. As a partially-sighted artist, Raffaella relies on sensory cues and touch through impasto and hand-painting techniques. She completed the Tracey Emin Artist Residency (TEAR) in 2023-24 and was announced as the Overall Winner of the Women in Art Prize in 2025.

Eric Ravilious 1903-1942 was a British painter and wood-engraver who was married to artist Tirzah Garwood. In 1922, he won a scholarship to the Royal College of Art, where he was encouraged to take up wood-engraving by his tutor, Paul Nash. In addition to watercolour paintings of landscapes and interiors, Ravilious regularly produced illustrations for books and objects, including Wedgwood ceramic commissions. From 1939, he served as a war artist, documenting ships, aircraft and coastal defences until his death aged 39, lost at sea off Iceland during a search-and-rescue mission.

Anne Redpath 1895-1965 was a Scottish artist known for still lifes and landscapes, inspired by her travels across Europe. Living in France between 1920 and 1934, she was influenced by Henri Matisse and Pierre Bonnard. After her return to Scotland, her work moved towards abstraction. She was President of the Scottish Society of Women Artists from 1944 to 1947 and became the first female painter admitted to the Royal Scottish Academy as an Academician in 1952.

Henri Rousseau 1844-1910 was a French, post-Impressionist painter nicknamed 'Le Douanier' (the customs officer) in reference to his previous career at a toll station. Following his early retirement in 1893, he turned to painting and exhibited regularly at the Salon des Indépendents. He was largely scorned by critics during his lifetime but found admirers in the likes of Guillaume Apollinaire, Fernand Léger and Pablo Picasso, who hosted 'Le Banquet Rousseau' in his honour in 1908.

William Scott 1913-1989 was an abstract painter from Northern Ireland known for his still lifes, landscapes and nudes produced over a 60-year period. While serving as a print draughtsman during the Second World War, he continued to exhibit paintings and subsequently took up a teaching position at Bath Academy of Art in 1946. He developed friendships with Mark Rothko and Willem de Kooning in 1953, bringing together both Abstract Expressionist and European figurative influences in his later work. He was the subject of a major retrospective at Tate Gallery in 1972.

Detail of Doron Langberg, *Hibiscus 1*, 2022

Judith Tucker 1960-2023 was a British artist and academic, known for her work concerning social history, memory and geography. She was a founding member of LAND2, a research network of artists and researchers interested in radical approaches to landscapes. She exhibited widely at home and abroad and was awarded a Jackson's Painting Prize (2020) and shortlisted for the Westmorland Landscape Prize (2019) and New Light Prize (2020-21). At the time of her death, she was Chair of Contemporary British Painting.

Euan Uglow 1932-2000 was a British painter, known for his precise nude and still-life paintings. He was a pupil of William Coldstream at both the Camberwell School of Art and Slade School of Art, where he later taught. During his lifetime, Uglow's work was the subject of retrospectives at the Whitechapel Gallery in 1974 and 1989 and featured in the group exhibition *Eight Figurative Painters* at the Yale Center for British Art in New Haven, Connecticut, in 1981-82.

Charlotte Verity born 1954 is a British painter and printmaker. Her garden, in southeast London and now Somerset, are the focus of her work and she often paints outside or brings elements of nature into her studio. She graduated from the Slade School of Art in 1977 and has undertaken residencies at Towner Eastbourne and the Garden Museum, London. Since 2001 she has taught at the Royal Drawing School.

Édouard Vuillard 1868-1940 was a French painter and decorative artist. He was a member of Les Nabis, an artistic group influenced by the bold colours of Paul Gauguin and Japanese woodblock prints. After the dissolution of Les Nabis in 1900, his style moved toward naturalism, a shift that was marked by an exhibition of interiors and landscapes at Galerie Bernheim-Jeune in 1908.

Caroline Walker born 1982 is a Scottish artist working in Dunfermline. Drawing from her own photographic source material, she is known for her representations of working women and sites of domestic labour. She obtained an MA in Painting from the Royal College of Art in 2009 and has since exhibited widely with notable solo exhibitions at KM21, The Hague (2021); Midlands Art Centre, Birmingham (2021); and K11 Art Foundation, Shanghai (2022). In 2025, her exhibition *Mothering* opened at Hepworth Wakefield, before travelling to Pallant House Gallery, Chichester, and Newlyn Art Gallery & The Exchange in 2026.

Alison Watt born 1965 won the 1987 John Player Portrait Award at the National Portrait Gallery while still a student at Glasgow School of Art. In 2000, she became the youngest artist to hold a major solo exhibition at the Scottish National Gallery of Art, which featured large paintings of fabric and marked a shift in her practice towards still life. In 2006-08 she was Associate Artist at the National Gallery, London. She was awarded an OBE in 2008 and became a Fellow of the Royal Society of Edinburgh in 2017.

Christopher Wood 1901-1930 left Liverpool for Paris in 1921 to study drawing at the Académie Julian, soon establishing himself in artistic circles where he mingled with members of the European avant-garde including Pablo Picasso and Jean Cocteau. Returning to Britain, he became a member of the Seven and Five Society and developed a close relationship with the artists Ben and Winifred Nicholson. After his tragic death, aged 29, Jim Ede organised a memorial exhibition of his work in 1932.

Clare Woods born 1972 trained as a sculptor but has dedicated herself to painting for the last 30 years. Influenced by Paul Nash and Barbara Hepworth, she is interested in translating physical forms into two-dimensional space. Her work has been the subject of solo exhibitions at the Hepworth Wakefield (2011) and Pallant House Gallery, Chichester (2016). In 2022, she was elected as a Royal Academician.

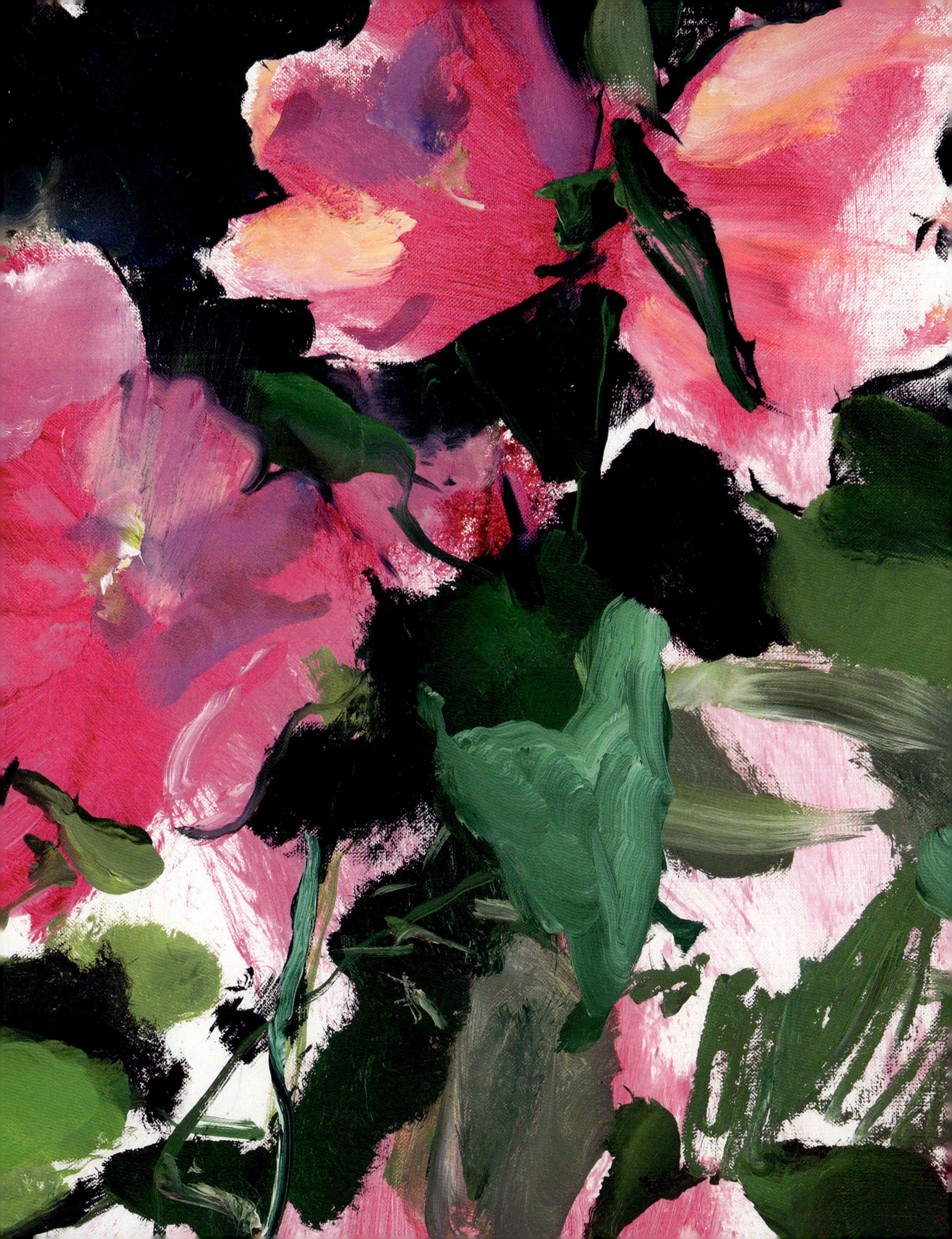

Image Credits

Kettle's Yard house 07
Photo: Jasper Fry. Courtesy Kettle's Yard

Hurvin Anderson 17
© Hurvin Anderson. Courtesy the artist and Thomas Dane Gallery. Photograph by Mark Dalton

Vanessa Bell 10,19
© Courtesy of the artist and Xavier Hufkens, Brussels. Photograph by Thomas Merle

David Bomberg 21
Courtesy Leeds Museums and Galleries © 2025 The Estate of David Bomberg. All Rights Reserved, DACS

Louise Bourgeois 23
Photo: Peter Butler, © 2026 The Easton Foundation/ VAGA at ARS, NY and DACS, London

Jai Chuhan 25
Courtesy the artist. Photograph by Peter Otto

Andrew Cranston 27
Courtesy the artist and Ingleby Gallery © Andrew Cranston

Kaye Donachie 29
© Kaye Donachie, courtesy Maureen Paley, London. Photograph by Stephen James

Gigi Ettedgui 31
Courtesy the artist

Anna Freeman Bentley 33
© Anna Freeman Bentley. Photograph by Anna Arca Photography

Marjory Garnett 35
© The Polar Museum, Scott Polar Research Institute

Tirzah Garwood 37
Courtesy of Dulwich Picture Gallery, London. Photograph by Alastair Innes

Gluck 15,39
Courtesy of The Fine Art Society Ltd © The artist's estate

Lubaina Himid 41
© Lubaina Himid. Courtesy Hollybush Gardens, London and Greene Naftali, New York. Photograph by Gavin Renshaw

Howard Hodgkin 43
© 2025 The Estate of Howard Hodgkin. All rights reserved, DACS Images

Isak of Igdlorpait 45
© The Polar Museum, Scott Polar Research Institute

Nerys Johnson 47
Courtesy of the artist's estate and Women's Art Collection, Murry Edwards College, Cambridge. Photograph by Mark Dalton

David Jones 49
© The Estate of David Jones. All Rights Reserved 2026 / Bridgeman Images. Photograph by Mark Dalton

Poppy Jones 51
© Poppy Jones. Courtesy the artist; Herald St, London; and Overduin & Co., Los Angeles. Photograph by Paul Salveson

Joy Labinjo 53
© Joy Labinjo. Courtesy Tiwani Contemporary. Photograph by Stuart Whipps

Doron Langberg 55, 115
© Doron Langberg. Courtesy the artist and Victoria Miro

Aubrey Levinthal 14, 57
© Aubrey Levinthal. Courtesy the artist and Ingleby Gallery. Photograph by John MaKenzie

Charles Rennie Mackintosh 12, 59
© The Hunterian, University of Glasgow

Rory McEwen 61
© Estate of Rory McEwen. Photograph by Mark Dalton

Cedric Morris 11, 63
Philip Mould & Company, London © The Estate of Cedric Morris. All Rights Reserved 2026 / Bridgeman Images

Cassi Namoda 65
© Courtesy of the artist and Xavier Hufkens, Brussels. Photograph by Thomas Merle

Mary Newcomb 67
© Estate of Mary Newcomb.
Courtesy Crane Kalman Gallery

William Nicholson 69
Courtesy Jonathan Clark Fine Art

Winifred Nicholson 71
© Trustees of Winifred Nicholson. Courtesy Crane Kalman Gallery

Chris Ofili 73
© Chris Ofili. Courtesy the artist and Victoria Miro

Jennifer Packer 75
© Jennifer Packer. Photograph © The Fitzwilliam Museum, University of Cambridge

Celia Paul 77
© Celia Paul. Courtesy Victoria Miro Gallery

Bryan Pearce 79
Courtesy of Jenna Burlingham Gallery, Hampshire and the artist's estate

Emma Prempeh 81
© Emma Prempeh. Courtesy of the artist and Tiwani Contemporary. Photograph by Deniz Guzel

Bianca Raffaella 3, 83
© Bianca Raffaella, courtesy Flowers Gallery, London/Hong Kong

Eric Ravilious 85
Courtesy of Towner Eastbourne

Anne Redpath 87
Aberdeen City Council (Aberdeen Archives, Gallery & Museums collections) © The Estate of Anne Redpath. All Rights Reserved 2026 / Bridgeman Images

Henri Rousseau 89
Bouquet of Flowers, circa1910, Henri Rousseau. Tate: Bequeathed by C. Frank Stoop 1933. Photo: Tate

William Scott 91
William Scott, Still Life - Flowers And Jug, 1946 © The artist's estate. Photo by Birmingham Museums Trust. Courtesy of Birmingham Museums Trust

Judith Tucker 93
© Estate of Judith Tucker. Photograph by Helen Clarke

Euan Uglow 95
Courtesy of Hazlitt Holland-Hibbert. © The Estate of Euan Uglow. All Rights Reserved 2026 / Bridgeman Images

Charlotte Verity 97, 119
© the artist. Photographer Ben Westoby

Édouard Vuillard 99
© The Fitzwilliam Museum, University of Cambridge

Caroline Walker 3, 101
© Caroline Walker. Courtesy the Artist; GRIMM, Amsterdam/New York/London; Ingleby Gallery, Edinburgh. Photo: Isla Macer Law

Alison Watt 103
© Alison Watt. Courtesy of Lévy Gorvy Dayan

Christopher Wood 105
© Pallant House Gallery, Chichester

Clare Woods 107
© Clare Woods. Courtesy the artist

Acknowledgments

In making the exhibition and this publication, we owe our gratitude to many institutions and individuals. We are especially grateful to: the lenders to the exhibition, public and private, for their vital support; to Olivia Meehan for sharing her knowledge and insights in her essay; to the artists and their estates for granting permission to reproduce the images; to the team at A Practice for Everyday Life, especially Kirsty Carter, Daniel Griffiths and Tom Young, for designing the exhibition graphics and other materials with consummate skill and sensitivity; to Eugenie Dodd and Karen Burbano for designing a beautiful book and being wonderful creative collaborators. Our special thanks are also due to the members of the Kettle's Yard Community Panel, especially Bryan Johnson, Abi Moore, Jade Pollard-Crowe and Alan Soer, for helping to shape and develop the exhibition from the beginning, ably supported by our colleague Karen Thomas, Community Manager. Throughout it has been a pleasure to work with the contemporary artists in the exhibition; we have greatly appreciated their interest and enthusiasm.

We have been fortunate in having the support and goodwill of the following who have each, in different ways, made exhibiting the work of 46 remarkable artists possible: Jane Adams, Mary Adams, Simon Adams, Maria Balshaw, Jane Bhoyroo, Axelle Blanc, Malcolm Chapman, Adrienne Chau, Jonathan Clark, Stamos Fafalios, Helen Fothergill, Penny Gluckstein, Amy de la Haye, Joe Hill, Christabel Holland, Beth Hughes, Florence Ingleby, Richard Ingleby, Isobel Jones, Andrew Kalman, Rachel Kent, Robin Light, Isla Macer Law, Jamie Mackinnon, Simon Martin, Zak Mensah, Laura Moseley, Philip Mould, Jovan Nicholson, Sophie Oppenheimer, Antony Peattie, Griselda Pollock, Kate Ravilious, Mark Ravilious, Olivia Rawnsley, Imogen Sampson, Veronica Sekules, Joseph Sharples, Virginia Sirena, Luke Syson, Harriet Tarlo, Nicola Togneri, Isabel Vegas, Sara Wajid and David Waterhouse.

An exhibition and book of this scope has required the creativity and hard work of the whole team at Kettle's Yard, especially Tom Allin-Roberts, Gabrielle Brasier, Lalie Constantin, Meri Croft, Helen Davies, Guy Haywood, Edie Ingleby, Tom Noblett, Laura Pryke, Tom Rowe and Ruby Salter. Finally, our ability to realise this exhibition and publication has relied on the generosity of many individual donors and other supporters. In particular, our warmest thanks go to Sally and Edward Benthall and to The Finnis Scott Foundation.

Megan Breckell, Andrew Nairne and Naomi Polonsky, April 2026

Detail of Charlotte Verity,
In the Green, 2021